FAI
FO(
GUIDE

First Edition 2001

Editors: Billy Heyman, Nick Woodworth &
Natasha Wladyka

Published by: **Fanfare Sporting Books**
                5th floor, Goldsmith house
                137-141 Regent Street
                London
                W1B 4HZ

Sales enquiries and orders:
Telephone: 020 7287 7053
Fax: 020 7287 7121

Printed and Bound in Great Britain by Livesey Printers Limited, Shrewsbury, Shropshire. SY3 9EB.

This Publication is protected by International Copyright law. All rights reserved. No part of this publication may be reproduced, stored in a retrieval system, or transmitted in any form or by any means, electronic, mechanical, photocopying, recording or otherwise, without prioir permission from the publisher.

ISBN :0-9541515-0-X

Acknowledgements:

Many thanks to the clubs, and the hundreds of you that helped us via message boards and emails, we are very grateful. Thankyou also to Chris Bruce-Payne, Marcus Lawler, Pete Manley, Caroline Carey and Dan Beattie for your ideas. Also to Mary Townsend for her creative flair. ....Save Chip!

Introduction

This pocket book is designed for the home fan, the away traveller and to people of all ages. We have tried to make it as timeless as we can in an attempt to extend the life of the book and to ensure you get best value and full enjoyment out of it. This guide was bourne out of the frustration of travelling to clubs by train, coach, car and occasionally by plane and not having the useful facts and directions easily to hand. It has been written as the name suggests, to fit in the pocket and be able to be taken to grounds without being overly cumbersome.

We have tried to visit every club and give factual information rather than opinion, although for interest we have put in Fanzines and Unofficial websites. Some of the facts listed you may disagree with; Nicknames, the year formed, and the capacities seem to vary on a monthly basis. What we have tried to do is list the most common answer from the hundreds of queries we have submitted.

My Rating:

The 'my rating box' has been designed to give the fan the ability to list their opinion in the book and to keep the guide as a personal reflection of their travels. We have intentionally designed it so that Children can also use it. We would be grateful if you submit your top 20 visited clubs by using the tear out slip at the back of the book, the results will then be compiled and reported in further editions.

We hope you enjoy the book.

Arsenal Football Club

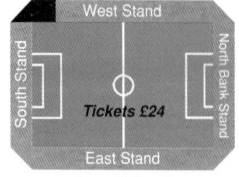

Address:
Arsenal Stadium
Avenell Road
Highbury
N5 1BU

Switch Board: 020 7704 4000
Ticket Office: 020 7704 4040
Website: www.arsenal.co.uk
Nickname: The Gunners
Year Formed: 1886
Record Attendance: 73,295 v Sunderland Mar, 1935
Record Receipts: £392,726.50 v Sampdoria April, 1995
Record League Victory: 12-0 v Loughborough Town Mar, 1900
Record Cup Victory: 11-1 v Darwen Jan, 1932
Record Defeat: 0-8 v Loughborough Town Dec, 1896
Most Capped Player: Kenny Sansom, England 77
Most League Appearances: David O'Leary, 558
Record Transfer Fee Received:
£22,900,000 for Nicolas Anelka, Aug 1999
Record Transfer Fee Paid:
£11,000,000 for Sylvain Wiltord, Aug 2000
Capacity: 38,500   **Fanzine:** The Gooner
Away Capacity: 2,900 **Unofficial site:** www.arsenal-world.net
Disabled places: 184

Last 5 Seasons:	Last 5 Managers:
1997: Prem - 3rd	Terry Neill (76-83)
1998: Prem - 1st	Don Howe (84-86)
1999: Prem - 2nd	George Graham (86-95)
2000: Prem - 2nd	Bruce Rioch (95-96)
2001: Prem - 2nd	Arsene Wenger (96-Pre)

Arsenal Football Club

Travel:

Rail: Finsbury Park (Kings Cross) 08457 484950

Tube: Arsenal (Piccadilly Line)

Bus: National Coach Enquiries 0870 6082608

Car:

North:

From M1 exit at A1 junction 2/3. The A1 merges for a stretch with A406. Keep to the A1, later Archway Road and then Holloway Road. Turn left onto A503 Seven Sisters Road and after 1 mile right onto the A1201 Blackstock Road which becomes Highbury Park. Turn right into Aubert Park and right again into Avenell Road.

North West:

From the M40 at junction 1 stay on the A40 for 13 miles and on the A40(M). At Paddington turn onto the A501. When the A501 becomes 1 Road turn left onto Baron Street, signposted as the route for the A1. Take the first right Lion Street and turn left onto the A1. At the Highbury and Islington roundabout, turn right onto St.Pauls Road and then left onto the A1201 Highbury Grove. Turn left into Aubert Park and right into Avenell Road.

West:

Approaching on the M4 turn left onto the A406 Gunnersbury Avenue at junction 2. At Hanger Lane turn right onto the A40. Then as route for **NorthWest**.

MY RATING

Date Visited: _____

Rating out of 10:

1 2 3 4 5 6 7 8 9 10

Note: _____

Arsenal Football Club

South West:

Stay on the M3 to end and continue on A316 to Hammersmith. Turn right onto A4 for 1.25 miles, left onto the A3220 Warwick Road and then onto the M41. At end turn onto A40(M) and then as route for North West.

East:

From the M11 turn off onto the A406 at junction 4, and then onto the A503. After Tottenham Hale tube station, turn left into Broad Lane and then back onto the A503 Seven Sisters Road. Turn left onto the A1201 Blackstock Road and then as route for North.

Honours:

FA Premier League: Champions: 1997-1998. Runners-up: 1998-1999, 1999-2000, 2000-2001.

Football League: Division 1. Champions: 1930-1931, 1932-1933, 1933-1934, 1934-1935, 1937-1938, 1947-1948, 1952-1953, 1970-1971, 1988-1989, 1990-1991. Runners-up: 1925-1926, 1931-1932, 1972-1973. Division 2. Runners-up: 1903-1904.

FA Cup: Winners: 1930, 1936, 1950, 1971, 1979, 1993, 1998. Runners-up: 1927, 1932, 1952, 1972, 1978, 1980, 2001.

Double performed: 1970-1971, 1997-1998.

Football League Cup: Winners: 1987, 1993. Runners-up: 1968, 1969, 1988.

European Competitions:

Fairs Cup: 1963-1964, 1969-1970 (winners), 1970-1971.

European Cup: 1971-1972, 1991-1992, 1998-1999, 1999-2000, 2000 -2001.

UEFA Cup: 1978-1979, 1981-1982, 1982-1983, 1996-1997, 1997-1998, 1999-2000 (runners-up).

European Cup-Winners' Cup: 1979-1980 (runners-up), 1993-1994 (winners), 1994-1995 (runners-up).

Aston Villa Football Club

Address:
Villa Park
Trinity Road
Birmingham
B6 6HE

Switch Board: 0121 327 2299
Ticket Office: 0121 327 5353
Website: www.avfc.co.uk
Nickname: The Villains
Year Formed: 1874-75
Record Attendance: 76,588 v Derby Mar, 1946
Record Receipts: £1,196,712 Portugal v Czech Rep Jun, 1996
Record League Victory: 12-2 v Accrington Stanley Mar, 1892
Record Cup Victory: 13-0 v Wednesbury Old Ath Oct, 1886
Record Defeat: 1-8 v Blackburn, February 1889
Most Capped Player: Paul McGrath, Republic of Ireland 51
Most League Appearances: Charlie Aitken, 561
Record Transfer Fee Received:
£12,600,000 for Dwight Yorke, Aug 1998
Record Transfer Fee Paid:
£9,500,000 for Juan Pablo Angel, Jan 2001
Capacity: 42,584 **Fanzine:** Heroes & Villains
Away Capacity: 2,900 **Unofficial site:** www.heroesandvillains.net
Disabled places: 40

Last 5 Seasons:	Last 5 Managers:
1997: Prem - 5th	Graham Taylor (87-90)
1998: Prem - 7th	Dr Jozef Venglos (90-91)
1999: Prem - 6th	Ron Atkinson (91-94)
2000: Prem - 6th	Brian Little (94-98)
2001: Prem - 8th	John Gregory (98-Pre)

Aston Villa Football Club

Travel:

Rail: Witton 08457 484950 (Birmingham New Street)

Bus: National Coach Enquiries 0870 6082608

Car:

North:

Leave M42 junction 7 onto M6. Exit M6 at junction 6 onto the A38 (M) Aston Expressway. Take first exit right onto Victoria Road. At roundabout take right exit into Witton Road for Villa Park.

South:

Take M1 to junction 19, then M6. At junction 6 turn onto the A38 (M). Then as route for North.

East:

Approaching on the M42, turn off at junction 8 and get onto the M6 heading towards Birmingham. Then as route for South.

MY RATING

Date Visited: _____

Rating out of 10:
1 2 3 4 5 6 7 8 9 10

Note: _____

Aston Villa Football Club

Honours:

FA Premier League: Runners-up: 1992-1993.

Football League: Division 1. Champions: 1893-1894, 1895-1896, 1896-1897, 1898-1899, 1899-1900, 1909-1910, 1980-1981. Runners-up: 1888-1889, 1902-1903, 1907-1908, 1910-1911, 1912-1913, 1913-1914, 1930-1931, 1932-1933, 1989-1990. Division 2. Champions: 1937-1938, 1959-1960. Runners-up: 1974-1975, 1987-1988. Division 3. Champions: 1971-1972.

FA Cup: Winners: 1887, 1895, 1897, 1905, 1913, 1920, 1957. Runners-up: 1892, 1924, 2000.

Double performed: 1896-1897.

Football League Cup: Winners: 1961, 1975, 1977, 1994, 1996. Runners-up: 1963, 1971.

European Competitions:

European Cup: 1981-1982 (winners), 1982-1983.

UEFA Cup: 1975-1976, 1977-1978, 1983-1984, 1990-1991, 1993-1994, 1994-1995, 1996-1997, 1997-1998, 1998-1999.

World Cup Championship: 1982.

European Super Cup: 1982-1983 (winners), 1982-1983.

Barnsley Football Club

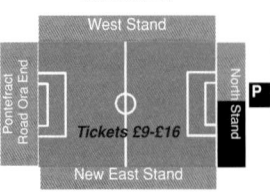

Grove Street

Address:
Oakwell Stadium
Grove Street
Barnsley
South Yorkshire, S71 1ET
Switch Board: 01226 211211
Ticket Office: 01226 211211
Website: www.barnsleyfc.co.uk
Nickname: Tykes
Year Formed: 1887

■ *Away Supporters*

Record Attendance: 40,255 v Stoke Feb, 1936
Record League Victory: 9-0 v Loughborough T Jan, 1899. v Accrington S Feb, 1934
Record Cup Victory: 6-0 v Blackpool Jan, 1910. v Peterborough U Sept, 1981
Record Defeat: 0-9 v Notts Co. Nov, 1927
Most Capped Player: Gerry Taggart, Northern Ireland 35
Most League Appearances: Barry Murphy, 514
Record Transfer Fee Received:
£4,250,000 for Ashley Ward, Dec 1998
Record Transfer Fee Paid:
£1,500,000 for Georgi Hristov, Jun 1997
Capacity: 23,009 **Fanzine:** Better Red Than Dead
Away Capacity: 6,000 Unofficial site: www.totaltykes.com
Disabled places: 91

Last 5 Seasons:	Last 5 Managers:
1997: Div 1, 2nd	Viv Anderson (93-94)
1998: Prem, 19th	Danny Wilson (94-98)
1999: Div 1, 13th	John Hendrie (98-99)
2000: Div 1, 4th	Dave Bassett (99-00)
2001: Div 1, 16th	Nigel Spackman (01-Pre)

Barnsley Football Club

Travel:

Rail: Barnsley 08457 484950

Bus: National Coach Enquiries 0870 6082608

Car:

From all Directions:

Leave the M1 at junction 37 and take the A628 towards Barnsley. After 400 meters you will come to some lights. Turn right following signs for the A6133 and Wakefield. Travel along the A6133 until you see the Coach and Horses pub at a crossroads. Turn left at the cross roads and then right at the lights into Oakwell Lane. At the end of the lane turn left then right and the ground is on the right.

Honours:

Football League: Division 1. Runners-up: 1996-1997. Division 3 (N). Champions: 1933-1934, 1938-1939, 1954-1955. Runners-up: 1953-1954. Division 3. Runners-up: 1980-1981. Division 4. Runners-up: 1967-1968. Promoted: 1978-1979.

FA Cup: Winners: 1912. Runners-up: 1910.

Football League Cup: Best season: 5th rd, 1982.

MY RATING

Date Visited: _____

Rating out of 10:

1 2 3 4 5 6 7 8 9 10

Note: _____

Birmingham City Football Club

Address:
St Andrew's
St Andrew's Street
Birmingham, B9 4NH
Switch Board: 0121 772 0101
Ticket Office: 07091 1125837
Website: www.bcfc.com
Nickname: The Blues
Year Formed: 1875

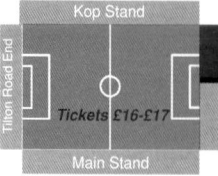

Record Attendance:
66,844 v Everton Feb, 1939
Record Receipts: £396,113 v Preston NE May, 2001
Record League Victory: 12-0 v Walsall T Swifts Dec, 1892
Record Cup Victory: 9-2 v Burton W Oct, 1885
Record Defeat: 1-9 v Sheffield W Dec, 1930
Most Capped Player: Malcolm Page, Wales 28
Most League Appearances: Frank Womack, 491
Record Transfer Fee Received:
£2,500,000 for Gary Breen, Jan 1997
Record Transfer Fee Paid:
£2,250,000 for Geoff Horsfield, July 2000
Capacity: 30,009   **Fanzine:** Singin The Blues
Away Capacity: 3,500 **Unofficial site:** www.keeprighton.co.uk
Disabled places: 90

Last 5 Seasons:	Last 5 Managers:
1997: Div 1 - 10th	Dave Mackay (89-91)
1998: Div 1 - 7th	Lou Macari (91)
1999: Div 1 - 4th	Terry Cooper (91-93)
2000: Div 1 - 5th	Barry Fry (93-96)
2000: Div 1 - 5th	Trevor Francis (96-Pre)

Birmingham City Football Club

Travel:

Rail: Bordesley (Birmingham New Street) 08457 484950

Bus: National Coach Enquiries 0870 6082608

Car:

From all Directions:

Leave the M6 at junction 6 and take the A38(M) (known locally as the Aston Expressway) for Birmingham City Centre. Continue past the first turn off (Aston, Waterlinks) and then take the next turn off, for the Inner Ring Road.

Turn left at the island at the top of the slip road and take the Ring Road East, signposted Coventry / Stratford. Continue along the ring road for two miles, crossing straight across three islands. At the fourth island (there is a large McDonalds on the far left hand corner) turn left towards Small Heath. Birmingham City's ground is about a 1/4 of a mile up this road on your left. The ground is also sign posted on the Inner Ring Road.

MY RATING

Date Visited: _____

Rating out of 10:

1 2 3 4 5 6 7 8 9 10

Note: _____

Birmingham City Football Club

Honours:

Football League: Division 1. Best season: 4th, 1998-1999. Division 2. Champions: 1892-1893, 1920-1921, 1947-1948, 1954-1955, 1994-1995. Runners-up: 1893-1894, 1900-1901, 1902-1903, 1971-1972, 1984-1985. Division 3. Runners-up: 1991-1992.

FA Cup: Runners-up: 1931, 1956.

Football League Cup: Winners: 1963, Runners-up 2001.

Leyland Daf Cup: Winners: 1991.

Auto Windscreens Shield: Winners: 1995.

European Competitions:

European Fairs Cup: 1955-1958, 1958-1960 (Runners-up), 1960-1961 (Runners-up), 1961-1962.

Blackburn Rovers Football Club

Address:
Ewood Park
Bolton Road
Blackburn
BB2 4JF

Switch Board: 01254 698888

Ticket Office: 01254 671666

Website: www.rovers.co.uk

Nickname: Rovers/Blue and Whites

Year Formed: 1875

Record Attendance: 62,522 v Bolton Wanderers Mar, 1929

Record Receipts: £438,868 v Newcastle U Jan, 2000

Record League Victory: 9-0 v Middlesbrough Nov, 1954

Record Cup Victory: 11-0 v Rossendale Oct, 1884

Record Defeat: 0-8 v Arsenal Feb, 1933

Most Capped Player: Bob Crompton, England 41

Most League Appearances: Derek Fazackerley, 596

Record Transfer Fee Received:
£15,000,000 for Alan Shearer, Jul 1996

Record Transfer Fee Paid:
£7,250,000 for Kevin Davies, Jun 1998

Capacity: 31,367   **Fanzine:** 4000 Holes

Away Capacity: 8,000 **Unofficial Site:** www.brfc-supporters.org.uk

Disabled places: 822

Last 5 Seasons:	Last 5 Managers:
1997: Prem - 13th	Ray Harford (95-97)
1998: Prem - 6th	Roy Hodgson (97-98)
1999: Prem - 19th	Brian Kidd (98-99)
2000: Div 1 - 11th	Tony Parkes (99-00)
2001: Div 1 - 2nd	Graeme Souness (00-Pre)

Blackburn Rovers Football Club

Travel:

Rail: Blackburn Central 08457 484950

Bus: National Coach Enquiries 0870 6082608

Car:

North:

Use the M6 to junction 30, then follow the M61 and leave at junction 9 which forms the M65 (signposted Blackburn). Leave the M65 at junction 4 (A666) and follow signs towards Blackburn. Ewood Park is about 1 mile down the road on the right hand side.

South:

Use M6 to junction 29, then onto the M65 towards Blackburn. Leave the M65 at junction 4 (A666) and follow signs towards Blackburn. Turn right at the first set of traffic lights and Ewood Park is about 1 mile down the road on the right hand side.

East:

Use M62 onto M66 (which becomes the A56), then onto the M65 (joining at junction 8), heading towards Blackburn. Leave the M65 at junction 4 (A666) and follow signs towards Blackburn. Then follow directions as if coming from the North.

MY RATING

Date Visited: _____

Rating out of 10:

1 2 3 4 5 6 7 8 9 10

Note: _____

Blackburn Rovers Football Club

Honours:

FA Premier League: Champions: 1994-1995. **Runners-up:** 1993-1994.

Football League: Division 1. Champions: 1911-1912, 1913-1914, **Runners-up** 2000-2001.

Division 2. Champions: 1938-1939. **Runners-up:** 1957-1958.
Division 3. Champions: 1974-1975. **Runners-up:** 1979-1980.

FA Cup: Winners: 1884, 1885, 1886, 1890, 1891, 1928. **Runners-up:** 1882, 1960.

Football League Cup: Semi-final 1962, 1993.

Full Members' Cup: Winners: 1987.

European Competitions:

European Cup: 1995-1996.

UEFA Cup: 1994-1995, 1998-1999.

Blackpool Football Club

Address:
Bloomfield Road
Blackpool
Lancashire, FY1 6JJ
Switch Board: 01253 405331
Ticket Office: 01253 405331
Website: www.blackpoolfc.co.uk
Nickname: Seasiders
Year Formed: 1887

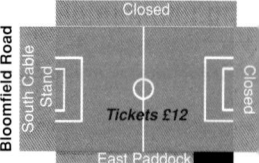

Record Attendance: 38,098 v Wolverhampton W Sep, 1955
Record Receipts: £79,420 v Preston NE Nov, 1998
Record League Victory: 7-0 v Reading Nov, 1928
Record Cup Victory: 7-1 v Charlton Ath Sep, 1963
Record Defeat: 1-10 v Small Heath Mar, 1901
Most Capped Player: Jimmy Armfield, England 43
Most League Appearances: Jimmy Armfield, 568
Record Transfer Fee Received:
£750,000 for Trevor Sinclair, Aug 1993
Record Transfer Fee Paid:
£275,000 for Chris Malkin, Oct 1996
Capacity: 6,100   **Fanzine:** Another View From the Tower
Away Capacity: 1,060 **Unofficial site:** www.blackpool-mad.co.uk
Disabled places: 12

Last 5 Seasons:	Last 5 Managers:
1997: Div 2 - 7th	Bill Ayre (90-94)
1998: Div 2 - 12th	Sam Allardyce (94-96)
1999: Div 2 - 14th	Gary Megson (96-97)
2000: Div 2 - 22nd	Nigel Worthington (97-99)
2001: Div 3 - 7th	Steve McMahon (00-Pre)

Blackpool Football Club

Travel:

Rail: Blackpool South Shore/Blackpool North 08457 484950

Bus: National Coach Enquiries 0870 6082608

Car:

From all Directions:

Follow the M6 to junction 32. At junction 32 exit onto the M55. Continue to the end of the motorway and carry straight on along Yeadon Way. Go straight over the first two roundabouts, then when you get to a mini-roundabout, turn right and the ground is 0.5 mile on the right.

If you are driving to the ground from the town/beach area, then head towards the tower along the sea front. Turn right off the Promenade then left onto Lytham Road. Continue until you get to some traffic lights, (you will be able to see the Old Bridge pub in front of you). Now turn right into Bloomfield Road and the ground is 200m on the left.

Honours:

Football League: Division 1. Runners-up: 1955-1956. Division 2: Champions: 1929-1930. Runners-up: 1936-1937, 1969-1970. Promoted from Division 3, 2000-2001 (play-offs) Division 4. Runners-up: 1984-1985.

FA Cup: Winners: 1953. Runners-up: 1948, 1951.

Football League Cup: Semi-final 1962. **Anglo-Italian Cup:** Winners: 1971. Runners-up: 1972.

MY RATING

Date Visited: _____

Rating out of 10:

1 2 3 4 5 6 7 8 9 10

Note: _____
_____
_____
_____

Bolton Wanderers Football Club

Address:
Reebok Stadium
Lostock
Bolton
BL6 6JW

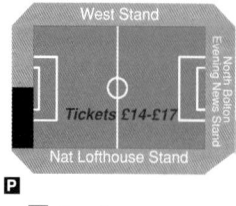

Away Supporters

Switch Board: 01204 673673
Ticket Office: 01204 673601
Website: www.bwfc.co.uk
Nickname: The Trotters
Year Formed: 1874
Record Attendance: 69,912 v Manchester City Feb, 1933
Record Receipts: £335,468 v WBA May, 2001
Record League Victory: 8-0 v Barnsley Oct, 1934
Record Cup Victory: 13-0 v Sheffield United Feb, 1890
Record Defeat: 1-9 v Preston NE Dec, 1887
Most Capped Player: Mark Fish, South Africa 34
Most League Appearances: Eddie Hopkinson, 519
Record Transfer Fee Received:
£4,500,000 for Jason McAteer, Sep 1995
Record Transfer Fee Paid:
£3,500,000 for Dean Holdsworth, Oct 1997
Capacity: 27,879   **Fanzine:** Tripe and Trotter
Away Capacity: 3,000 **Unofficial site:** www.bwsa.cwc.net
Disabled places: 250

Last 5 Seasons:	Last 5 Managers:
1997: Div 1 - 1st	Phil Neal (85-92)
1998: Prem - 18th	Bruce Rioch (92-95)
1999: Div 1 - 6th	Roy McFarland (95-96)
2000: Div 1 - 6th	Colin Todd (96-99)
2001: Div 1 - 3rd	Sam Allardyce (99-Pre)

Bolton Wanderers Football Club

Travel:

Rail: Horwich Parkway
08457 484950

Bus: National Coach
Enquiries 0870 6082608

Car: North:

Follow the M6 to junction 29 and take the M65 towards Blackburn. Leave the M65 at junction 2 and join the M61 towards Manchester. Leave the M61 at junction 6 and the ground is visible from this junction and is clearly sign posted. Ensure that when approaching the ground you look out for the home and away car parks, they are seperate.

South: Follow the M6 to junction 21a, take the Eastbound M62 signposted for Manchester leaving at junction 12. Having joined the M60 follow signs for M61 (Bolton/Preston) and leave the M61 motorway at junction 6. The ground is visible from this junction and is clearly signposted. Ensure that when approaching the ground you look out for the home and away car parks; they are in separate locations.

MY RATING

Date Visited: _____

Rating out of 10:

1 2 3 4 5 6 7 8 9 10

Note: _____

Honours:

Football League: Division 1. Champions: 1996-1997. Promoted from Division 1 (play offs) 2000-2001. Division 2. Champions: 1908-1909, 1977-1978. Runners-up: 1899-1900, 1904-1905, 1910-1911, 1934-1935, 1992-1993. Division 3. Champions: 1972-1973.

FA Cup: Winners: 1923, 1926, 1929, 1958. Runners-up: 1894, 1904, 1953.

Football League Cup: Runners-up: 1995.

Bournemouth Football Club

Address:
Dean Court
Bournemouth
Dorset, BH7 7AF
Switch Board: 01202 395381
Ticket Office: 01202 397939
Website: www.afcb.co.uk
Nickname: The Cherries
Year Formed: 1899

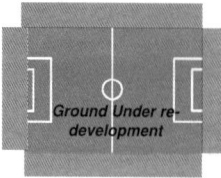

Record Attendance: 28,799 v Manchester United Mar, 1957
Record Receipts: £80,267 v Walsall Mar, 1998
Record league Victory: 7-0 v Swindon T Sep, 1956
Record Cup Victory: 11-0 v Margate Nov, 1971
Record Defeat: 0-9 v Lincoln City Dec, 1982
Most Capped Player: Gerry Peyton, Republic of Ireland 7
Most League Appearances: Sean O'Driscoll, 423
Record Transfer Fee Received:
£800,000 for Joe Parkinson, Mar 1989
Record Transfer Fee Paid:
£210,000 for Gavin Peacock, Aug 1989
Capacity: 12,000   **Fanzine:** Community Service
Away Capacity: 2,600 **Unofficial site:** www.botw.co.uk
Disabled places: 30

Last 5 Seasons:	Last 5 Managers:
1997: Div 2 - 16th	Don Megson (83)
1998: Div 2 - 9th	Harry Redknapp (83-92)
1999: Div 2 - 7th	Tony Pulis (92-94)
2000: Div 2 - 16th	Mel Machin (94-00)
2000: Div 2 - 7th	Sean O'Driscoll (00-Pre)

Bournemouth Football Club

Travel:

Rail: Pokesdown or Bournemouth Central 08457 484950

Bus: National Coach Enquiries 0870 6082608

Car:

North or East:

Follow the A338 towards Bournemouth. The ground is situated on the left of the A338 in the outskirts of Bournemouth. If you keep looking up to the left as you go into Bournemouth you will eventually see the tops of the ground floodlights. At this point take the next exit off the A338 and turn left towards the ground.

West:

Follow the A348 and then turn left onto the A3049 through Bournemouth. Continue until you cross the A338 Wessex Way dual carriageway. At the next roundabout turn left into Holdenhurst Road, and at the following roundabout take the third exit into Littledown Avenue. Take the next exit signposted King's Park, then immediately turn right into Thistlebarrow Road.

During the 2001/2002 season, Bournemouth will be playing at Dorchester Town's Avenue Stadium:

From all directions follow the A35 Dorchester by-pass. Ignore the signs for the Town Centre, at the junction/roundabout with the A354 (Weymouth) turn off onto the B3147. The Stadium floodlights will now be visible. Turn 1st right into Tesco's and the Avenue Stadium is situated on your right.

MY RATING

Date Visited: _____

Rating out of 10:

1 2 3 4 5 6 7 8 9 10

Note: _____

Bournemouth Football Club

Honours:

Football League: Division 3. Champions: 1986-1987. Division 3 (S). Runners-up: 1947-1948. Division 4. Runners-up: 1970-1971. Promotion from Division 4: 1981-1982 (4th).

FA Cup: Best season: 6th rd, 1957.

Football League Cup: Best season: 4th rd, 1962, 1964.

Associate Members' Cup: Winners: 1984.

Auto Windscreens Shield: Runners-up: 1998.

Bradford City Football Club

Address:
Bradford & Bingley Stadium
Valley Parade
Bradford
West Yorkshire, BD8 7DY
Switch Board: 01274 773355
Ticket Office: 01274 770022
Website: www.bradfordcityfc.co.uk

Nickname: The Bantams

Year Formed: 1903

Record Attendance: 39,146 v Burnley Mar, 1911

Record Receipts: £164,567 v Sheffield Wednesday Feb, 1997

Record League Victory: 11-1 v Rotherham U Aug, 1928

Record Cup Victory: 11-3 v Walker Celtic Dec, 1937

Record Defeat: 1-9 v Colchester Dec, 1961

Most Capped Player: Harry Hampton, Northern Ireland 9

Most League Appearances: Cec Podd, 502

Record Transfer Fee Received:
2,000,000 for Des Hamilton, Mar 1997

Record Transfer Fee Paid:
2,500,000 for David Hopkin, Jul 2000

Capacity: 25,000 **Fanzine:** The City Gent

Away Capacity: 3500 **Unofficial site:** www.boyfrombrazil.co.uk

Disabled places: 16

Last 5 Seasons:	Last 5 Managers:
1997: Div 1 - 21st	Lennie Lawrence (94-95)
1998: Div 1 - 13th	Chris Kamara (95-98)
1999: Div 1 - 2nd	Paul Jewell (98-00)
2000: Prem - 17th	Chris Hutchings (00)
2001: Prem - 20th	Jim Jefferies (00-Pre)

Bradford City Football Club

Travel:

Rail: Forster Square 08457 484950

Bus: National Coach Enquiries 0870 6082608

Car:

North: Take the A650 signposted for Bradford. Turn left onto the outer Ring Rd then take the first right turn by the hospital into the Midland Rd. The ground is then about half a mile on the right.

South: Leave the M62 at junction 26 onto the M606. The M606 ends at The Odsal Top roundabout. Take the last exit (past McDonalds on the left) into Rooley Lane (signposted Airport). At the second roundabout turn left into A650 Wakefield Rd. Cross two more roundabouts as Wakefield Rd becomes Shipley Airedale Rd and then Canal Rd. As the road goes down the hill you can see the stadium on the left. Just after Staples Office Equipment (on left) turn left into Station Rd and left again into Queens Rd. Continue up the hill and at the third set of lights turn left into Manningham Lane. After the petrol station on the left take the first left into Valley Parade

East/West: M62 to J26, then on to the M606. Follow directions as if travelling South.

Honours:

Football League: Division 1. Runners-up: 1998-1999. Division 2 Champions 1907-1908. Promoted from Division 2: 1995-1996 (play-offs). Division 3. Champions: 1984-1985. Division 3 (N). Champions: 1928-1929. Division 4. Runners-up: 1981-1982.

FA Cup: Winners: 1911.

Football League Cup: Best season: 5th rd, 1965, 1989.

MY RATING

Date Visited: _____

Rating out of 10:

1 2 3 4 5 6 7 8 9 10

Note: _____

Brentford Football Club

Address:
Griffin Park
Braemar Road
Brentford
Middlesex, TW8 0NT

Switch Board: 020 8847 2511
Ticket Office: 020 8847 2511
Website: www.brentfordfc.co.uk

Nickname: The Bees

Year Formed: 1893

Record Attendance: 38,678 v Leicester Feb, 1949
Record Receipts: £162,314 v Tottenham H Sep, 1998
Record League Victory: 9-0 v Wrexham Oct, 1963
Record Cup Victory: 7-0 v Windsor & Eton Nov, 1982
Record Defeat: 0-7 v Swansea T Nov, 1924
Most Capped Player: John Buttigieg, Malta 22
Most League Appearances: Ken Coote, 514
Record Transfer Fee Received:
720,000, for Dean Holdsworth, Aug 92
Record Transfer Fee Paid:
850,000 for Hermann Hreidarsson, Sep 1998
Capacity: 12,763   **Fanzine:** Hey Jude
Away Capacity: Varies **Unofficial site:** www.saffrey.co.uk/brentford
Disabled places: 9

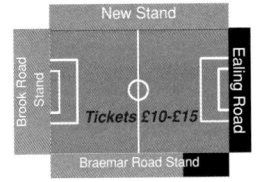

Away Supporters

Last 5 Seasons:	Last 5 Managers:
1997: Div 2 - 4th	Phil Holder (90-93)
1998: Div 2 - 21st	David Webb (93-97)
1999: Div 3 - 1st	Micky Adams (97-98)
2000: Div 2 - 17th	Ron Noades (98-00)
2001: Div 2 - 14th	Steve Coppell (01-Pre)

Brentford Football Club

Travel:

Rail: Brentford 08457 484950

Tube: South Ealing (Piccadilly Line)

Bus: National Coach Enquiries 0870 6082608

Car:

North, East:

Take the A406 North Circular Road to Chiswick. At the Chiswick Roundabout take the third exit onto Great West Road and continue straight on for three quarters of a mile before turning left on to the A3001 Ealing Road. The ground is half a mile on the right.

West:

Leave the M4 at junction 2 and take the A4 going around Chiswick roundabout so that you end up coming back on yourself. After a short distance turn left (Texaco Garage) onto the B455 (Ealing Road). Continue over the railway and the ground is on your right.

South:

Take the A205 South Circular Road (heading west) until you cross the river. Turn left into Kew Bridge Road (A315). Turn right after a quarter of a mile into Ealing Road (A3001) and the ground is a quarter of a mile on the left.

MY RATING

Date Visited: _____

Rating out of 10:

1 2 3 4 5 6 7 8 9 10

Note: _____

Brentford Football Club

Honours:

Football League: Division 1. Best season: 5th, 1935-1936. Division 2: Champions: 1934-1935. Division 3. Champions: 1991-1992, 1998-1999. Division 3 (S). Champions: 1932-1933, Runners-up: 1929-1930, 1957-1958. Division 4. Champions: 1962-1963.

FA Cup: Best season: 6th rd, 1938, 1946, 1949, 1989.

Football League Cup: Best season: 4th rd, 1983.

Freight Rover Trophy: Runners-up: 1985.

LDV Vans Trophy: Runners-up 2001.

Brighton & Hove Albion Football Club

Address:
Withdean Stadium
Tongdean Lane
Brighton
East Sussex, BN1 5JD
Switch Board: 01273 778855
Ticket Office: 01273 778855
Website: www.seagulls.co.uk
Nickname: Seagulls
Year Formed: 1901

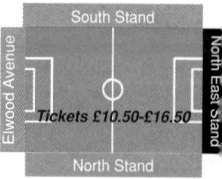

■ *Away Supporters*

Record Attendance: 36,747 v Fulham Dec, 1958
Record Receipts: £109,615.65 v Crawley T Jan, 1992
Record league Victory: 9-1 v Newport Co Apr, 1951
Record Cup Victory: 10-1 v Wisbech Nov, 1965
Record Defeat: 0-9 v Middlesbrough Aug, 1958
Most Capped Player: Steve Penney, Northern Ireland 17
Most League Appearances: "Tug" Wilson, 509
Record Transfer Fee Received:
£900,000 for Mark Lawrenson, Aug 1981
Record Transfer Fee Paid:
£500,000 for Andy Ritchie, Oct 1980
Capacity: 6,960   **Fanzine:** Keep the Faith
Away Capacity: 756   **Unofficial site:** www.total-albion.com
Disabled places: 86

Last 5 Seasons:	Last 5 Managers:
1997: Div 3 - 23rd	Jimmy Case (95-96)
1998: Div 3 - 23rd	Steve Gritt (96-98)
1999: Div 3 - 17th	Brian Horton (98-99)
2000: Div 3 - 11th	Jeff Wood (99)
2001: Div 3 - 1st	Micky Adams (99-Pre)

Brighton & Hove Albion Football Club

Travel:

Rail: Preston Park 08457 484950

Bus: National Coach Enquiries 0870 6082608

Car:

North: Head South down the A23 signposted for Brighton. As you head into Brighton you get to a junction with the A27. Turn off at Patcham and drive up Mill Road. There is no parking allowed within a mile of the ground, due to matchday restrictions and as a result, there is an excellent park and ride scheme which is available at Mill Road. Your match ticket includes a park and ride ticket for either train or bus.

East: Having travelled along the A26 join the A27 at Lewes. Continue to the A23 junction where you should turn left on to the A23 (signposted Brighton). Then drive as if travelling North.

West: Follow the A27 until you come to the junction with the A23. Turn right on to the A23 (signposted Brighton) then drive as if travelling North.

Honours:

Football League: Division 1. Best season: 13th, 1981-1982. Division 2: Runners-up: 1978-1979. Division 3 (S). Champions: 1957-1958, Runners-up: 1953-1954, 1955-1956. Division 3: Champions 2000 -2001, Runners-up: 1971-1972, 1976-1977, 1987-1988. Division 4. Champions: 1964-1965.

FA Cup: Runners-up, 1983.

Football League Cup: Best season: 5th rd, 1979.

MY RATING

Date Visited: _____

Rating out of 10:

1 2 3 4 5 6 7 8 9 10

Note: _____
_____
_____
_____

Bristol City Football Club

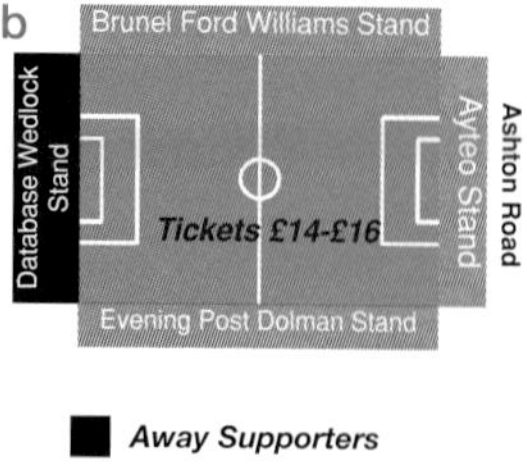

Address:
Ashton Gate
Winterstoke Road
Bristol
BS3 2JE
Switch Board: 0117 963 0630
Ticket Office: 0117 963 0630
Website: www.bcfc.co.uk
Nickname: The Robins
Year Formed: 1894
Record Attendance: 43,335 v Preston NE Feb, 1935
Record Receipts: £251,612 v Everton Jan, 1999
Record League Victory: 9-0 v Aldershot Dec, 1946
Record Cup Victory: 11-0 v Chichester C Nov, 1960
Record Defeat: 0-9 v Coventry C Apr, 1934
Most Capped Player: Billy Wedlock, England 26
Most League Appearances: John Atyeo, 597
Record Transfer Fee Received:
£3,000,000 for Ade Akinbiyi, Sep 1999
Record Transfer Fee Paid:
£1,200,000 for Ade Akinbiyi, May 1998
Capacity: 21,479   **Fanzine:** One Team in Bristol
Away Capacity: 5,500 **Unofficial site:** www.bristolcitynet.co.uk
Disabled places: 50

Tickets £14-£16

Away Supporters

Last 5 Seasons:	Last 5 Managers:
1997: Div 2 - 5th	John Ward (97-98)
1998: Div 2 - 2nd	Benny Lennartsson (98-99)
1999: Div 1 - 24th	Tony Pulis (99)
2000: Div 2 - 9th	Tony Fawthrop (00)
2001: Div 2 - 9th	Danny Wilson (00-Pre)

Bristol City Football Club

Travel:

Rail: Parson Street / Bristol Temple Meads 08457 484950

Bus: National Coach Enquiries 0870 6082608

Car: North, West: Travel down the M5 to junction 16. Pick up the A38 (signposted Patchway). Keep driving along the A38 and follow signs for Taunton. After crossing the river, bear left into Winterstoke Road, then turn left into Marsh Road and right into Ashton Road.

East: From the M4, come off at junction 19 and take the M32 into Bristol City Centre. Join the A38 and having followed the signs for Taunton travel as if going North / West.

South: From the M5 come off at junction 18. Take the left fork for the A4 and continue along the road crossing the swing bridge (Brunel Way). Bear left into Winterstoke Road and then travel as if going North / West.

Honours: Football League: Division 1. Runners-up: 1906-1907. Division 2. Champions: 1905-1906. Runners-up: 1975-1976, 1997-1998. Division 3 (S). Champions: 1922-1923, 1926-1927, 1954-1955. Runners-up: 1937-1938. Division 3. Runners-up: 1964-1965, 1989-1990.

FA Cup: Runners-up: 1909.

Football League Cup: Semi-final 1971, 1989.

Welsh Cup: Winners: 1934. **Anglo-Scottish Cup:** Winners: 1978. **Freight Rover Trophy:** Winners: 1986. Runners-up: 1987. **Auto Windscreens Shield:** Runners-up: 2000.

MY RATING

Date Visited: _____

Rating out of 10:

1 2 3 4 5 6 7 8 9 10

Note: _____

Bristol Rovers Football Club

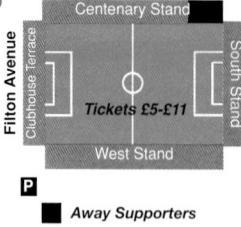

Address:
Memorial Stadium
Filton Avenue
Horfield
Bristol
BS7 0AQ
Switch Board: 0117 924 7474
Ticket Office: 0117 924 7474
Website: www.bristolrovers.co.uk
Nickname: The Pirates
Year Formed: 1883
Record Attendance: 11,433 v Sunderland Oct, 2000
Record Receipts: £115,000 v Sunderland Oct, 2000
Record League Victory: 7-0 v Brighton & HA Nov, 1952
Record Cup Victory: 6-0 v Merthyr Tydfil Nov, 1987
Record Defeat: 0-12 v Luton T Apr, 1936
Most Capped Player: Neil Slatter, Wales 10
Most League Appearances: Stuart Taylor, 546
Record Transfer Fee Received:
£2,000,000 for Barry Hayles, Nov 1998. Jason Roberts, Jul 2000
Record Transfer Fee Paid:
£370,000 for Andy Tillson Nov, 1992
Capacity: 11,976   **Fanzine:** Black Arab
Away Capacity: 1,100
Unofficial site: www.bristolroversonline.co.uk
Disabled places: 30

Last 5 Seasons:	Last 5 Managers:
1997: Div 2 - 17th	Malcolm Allision (92-93)
1998: Div 2 - 5th	John Ward (93-96)
1999: Div 2 - 13th	Ian Holloway (96-01)
2000: Div 2 - 7th	Gary Thompson (01)
2001: Div 2 - 21st	Gerry Francis (01-Pre)

Bristol Rovers Football Club

Travel:

Rail: Filton or Stapleton Road 0845 7 484950

Bus: National Coach Enquiries 0870 6082608

Car:

North:

M5 to junction 16 and join the A38 (South) towards Bristol City Centre. The ground is about five miles down the A38. You will pass the large British Aerospace works and further on you will pass on your left the Royal George and Duke Of York pubs. At the next traffic lights, the Memorial Ground is signposted to the left and is about 100 yards down this road.

East:

M4 to junction 19 and then take the M32 to junction 2. Take the fourth exit from the roundabout, signposted to the A38, bear right at fork into Muller Road B4469. Bear immediately right then continue for approximately one mile following signs to Horfield and Southmead until you see a church on your right-hand side. Take the second turning left into Filton Avenue.

South:

Take the A37 into Bristol and continue straight on to A4. Turn right onto the A4044 Temple Way, travel for one mile before taking the A4032 Newfoundland Street (following the signs for M32). Follow the M32 to junction 2, turn left onto Muller Road, then continue as if travelling East.

MY RATING

Date Visited: _____

Rating out of 10:

1 2 3 4 5 6 7 8 9 10

Note: _____

Bristol Rovers Football Club

Honours:

Football League: Division 2. Best season: 4th, 1994-1995. Division 3 (S). Champions: 1952-1953. Division 3. Champions: 1989-1990. Runners-up: 1973-1974.

FA Cup: Best season: 6th rd, 1951, 1958.

Football League Cup: Best season: 5th rd, 1971, 1972.

Burnley Football Club

Address:
Turf Moor
Harry Potts Way
Burnley
Lancashire, BB10 4BX

Switch Board: 01282 700000

Ticket Office: 01282 700000

Website:
www.burnleyfootballclub.com

Nickname: The Clarets

Year Formed: 1882

Record Attendance: 54,775 v Huddersfield T Feb, 1924

Record Receipts: £183,000 v Preston NE Mar, 2000

Record League Victory: 9-0 v Darwen Jan, 1892

Record Cup Victory: 9-0 v Crystal Palace Feb, 1909

Record Defeat: 0-10 v Aston Villa Jan, 1929

Most Capped Player: Jimmy McIlroy, Northern Ireland 51

Most League Appearances: Jerry Dawson, 522

Record Transfer Fee Received:
£750,000 for Steve Davis, Aug 1995

Record Transfer Fee Paid:
£1,000,000 for Ian Moore, Oct 2000

Capacity: 22,546   **Fanzine:** The Claret Flag

Away Capacity: 4,245 **Unofficial site:** www.claretsmad.co.uk

Disabled places: 52

Last 5 Seasons:	Last 5 Managers:
1997: Div 2 - 9th	Frank Casper (89-91)
1998: Div 2 - 20th	Jimmy Mullen (91-96)
1999: Div 2 - 15th	Adrian Heath (96-97)
2000: Div 2 - 2nd	Chris Waddle (97-98)
2001: Div 1 - 7th	Stan Ternent (98-Pre)

Burnley Football Club

Travel:

Rail: Burnley Central
08457 484950

Bus: National Coach
Enquiries 0870 6082608

Car:

North:

Leave the M6 at junction 29 and onto the M65. Leave the M65 at junction 10 and take the 5th exit (signposted Burnley A671). At the next roundabout you turn left onto Westway. At the traffic lights turn right (sign posted Burnley FC) into Trafalgar St. At the double roundabout at the bottom follow signs for A671 (towards Rochdale) onto A682 Centenary Way. At the next roundabout turn right (third exit) onto A671 follow the road under Culver Bridge and then across the traffic lights into Brunshaw Road.

East:

Take the A646 to A671 then travel along Todmorden Road towards the town centre. At the traffic lights turn right into Brunshaw Road where you will be able to see the ground

South/West:

Leave the M6 at junction 29 onto the M65 and then drive as if travelling **North**.

MY RATING

Date Visited: _____

Rating out of 10:

1 2 3 4 5 6 7 8 9 10

Note: _____

Burnley Football Club

Honours:

Football League: Division 1. Champions: 1920-1921, 1959-1960. **Runners-up:** 1919-1920, 1961-1962. **Division 2. Champions:** 1897-1898, 1972-1973. **Runners-up:** 1912-1913, 1946-1947, 1999-2000. Promoted from Division 2, 1993-1994 (play-offs). **Division 3. Champions:** 1981-1982. **Division 4. Champions:** 1991-1992. Record 30 consecutive Division 1 games without defeat 1920-1921.

FA Cup: Winners: 1914: **Runners-up:** 1947, 1962.

Football League Cup: Semi-final: 1961, 1969, 1983.

Anglo-Scottish Cup: Winners: 1979.

Sherpa Van Trophy: Runners-up: 1988.

European Competitions:

European Cup: 1960-1961.

European Fairs Cup: 1966-1967.

Bury Football Club

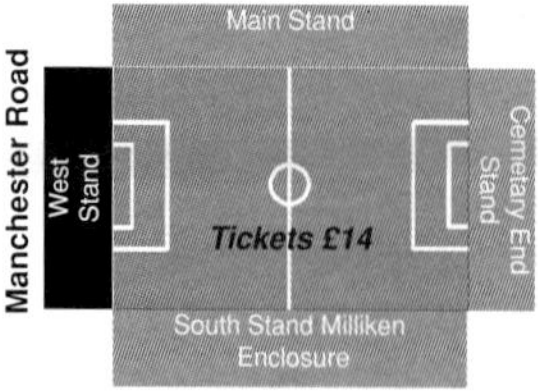

Address:
Gigg Lane
Bury
Lancashire
BL9 9HR
Switch Board: 0161 7644881
Ticket Office: 0161 7644881
Website: www.buryfc.co.uk
Nickname: The Shakers
Year Formed: 1885
Record Attendance: 35,000 v Bolton W Jan, 1960
Record Receipts: £86,000 v Manchester C Sep, 1997
Record League Victory: 8-0 v Tranmere R Jan, 1970
Record Cup Victory: 12-1 v Stockton Feb, 1897
Record Defeat: 0-10 v West Ham U Oct, 1983
Most Capped Player: Bill Gorman, Ireland 11
Most League Appearances: Norman Bullock, 506
Record Transfer Fee Received:
£1,100,000 for David Johnson, Nov 1997
Record Transfer Fee Paid:
£200,000 for Chris Swailes, Nov 1997. Darren Bullock, Feb 1999
Capacity: 11,669   **Fanzine:** Bury Me In White
Away Capacity: 2,600 **Unofficial site:** www.y3kshakers.com
Disabled places: 25

Last 5 Seasons:	Last 5 Managers:
1997: Div 2 - 1st	Sam Ellis (89-90)
1998: Div 1 - 17th	Mike Walsh (90-95)
1999: Div 1 - 22nd	Stan Ternent (95-98)
2000: Div 2 - 15th	Neil Warnock (98-99)
2001: Div 2 - 16th	Andy Preece (00-Pre)

Bury Football Club

Travel:

Rail: Bury Interchange 08457 484950

Bus: National Coach Enquiries 0870 6082608

Car:

North:

Take the M66 to junction 3. Exit at junction 3 and turn right onto Pilsworth Road heading towards the A56. Go straight on at the first roundabout. At the traffic lights turn right for the A56 onto Manchester Road. Go straight on through the first set of traffic lights and Gigg Lane is on the right

South, East and West:

Take M62/M60 to junction 18 and then take the M66 to junction 3. Turn left onto the Pilsworth Road and then follow the directions as if travelling from the North.

Honours:

Football League: Division 1. Best Season 1925 -1926, 4th.
Division 2: Champions: 1894-1895, 1996-1997; Runners-up 1923-1924; Division 3: Champions 1960-1961; Runners-up 1967-1968; Promoted from Division 3 (3rd) 1995-1996.

FA Cup: Winners 1900, 1903.

Football League Cup: Semi-final 1963.

MY RATING

Date Visited: _____

Rating out of 10:

1 2 3 4 5 6 7 8 9 10

Note: _____

Cambridge United Football Club

Address:
The Abbey Stadium
Newmarket Road
Cambridge
CB5 8LN

Switch Board: 01223 566500
Ticket Office: 01223 566500
Website: www.cambridge-united.co.uk
Nickname: The U's
Year Formed: 1912

Away Supporters

Record Attendance: 14,000 v Chelsea May, 1970
Record Receipts: £86,308 v Manchester U Oct, 1991
Record League Victory: 6-0 v Darlington Sep, 1971
Record Cup Victory: 5-1 v Bristol Feb, 1990
Record Defeat: 0-6 v Aldershot Apr. 1974 v Chelsea 1983. v Brentford 1995.
Most Capped Player: Tom Finney, Northern Ireland 7
Most League Appearances: Steve Spriggs, 416
Record Transfer Fee Received:
£1,000,000 for Dion Dublin, Aug 1992
Record Transfer Fee Paid:
£190,000 for Steve Claridge, Nov 1992
Capacity: 9,247   **Fanzine:** One Wonky Antler
Away Capacity: 2,100 **Unofficial site:** www.cambridgeunited.net
Disabled places: 18

Last 5 Seasons:	Last 5 Managers:
1997: Div 3 - 10th	Ian Atkins (92-93)
1998: Div 3 - 16th	Gary Johnson (93-95)
1999: Div 3 - 2nd	Tommy Taylor (95-96)
2000: Div 2 - 19th	Roy McFarland (96-01)
2001: Div 2 - 19th	John Beck (01-Pre)

Cambridge United Football Club

Travel:

Rail: Cambridge 08457 484950

Bus: National Coach Enquiries 0870 6082608

Car:

From North and West:

Follow the A14 towards Cambridge. After the A14 and M11 divides, stay on the A14 to the third exit (signposted Cambridge B1047).
Turn right at the T-junction at the end of the traffic lights (signposted Fen Ditton, Cambridge Airport). Follow this road through Fen Ditton to the next T-junction at a set of traffic lights. Turn right here (signposted Cambridge). Straight on at the roundabout after 100 yards (signposted ring road) into Newmarket Road. The ground is on the left after approximately 0.5 miles.

From South:

Leave the M11 at junction 11 (signposted Cambridge A1309). Turn right at the roundabout (signposted Cambridge A1309). Go straight on for 1.5 miles through three sets of traffic lights, then right at the next set of lights (signposted ring road) into Long Road. Straight on at the next lights (signposted ring road) into Queen Edith's Way. Follow 'ring road' signs at the next five roundabouts into Newmarket Road. The ground is on the left after approximately 0.5 miles.

From East:

Leave A14 at A1303 (signposted Cambridge A1303, Burwell B1102). Turn left at the roundabout (signposted Cambridge A1303). Continue straight on for 2.4 miles, over a roundabout, through two sets of traffic lights then across another roundabout. The ground is on the left after approximately 0.5 miles.

MY RATING

Date Visited: _____

Rating out of 10:

1 2 3 4 5 6 7 8 9 10

Note: _____

Cambridge United Football Club

Honours:

Football League: Division 2. Best season: 5th, 1991-1992. Division 3. Champions: 1990-1991. Runners-up: 1977-1978, 1998-1999. Division 4. Champions 1976-1977. Promoted from Divison 4 1989-1990 (play-offs).

FA Cup: Best season: 6th rd, 1990, 1991.

Football League Cup: Best season: 5th rd, 1993.

Cardiff City Football Club

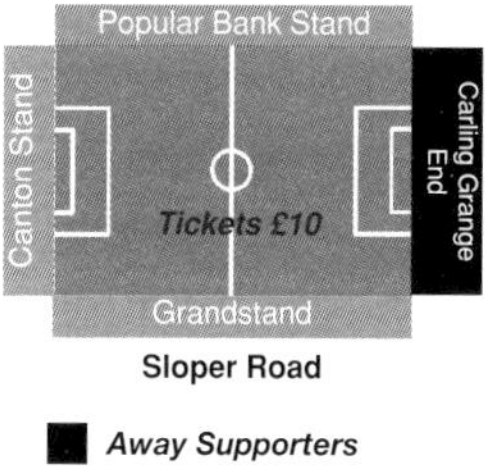

Address:
Ninian Park
Sloper Road
Cardiff
CF1 8SX

Switch Board: 02920 221001
Ticket Office: 02920 222857
Website: www.cardiffcityfc.co.uk
Nickname: The Bluebirds
Year Formed: 1899
Record Attendance: 62,634 Wales v England Oct, 1959
Record Receipts: £141,756 v Manchester C Jan, 1994
Record League Victory: 9-2 v Thames Feb, 1932
Record Cup Victory: 8-0 v Enfield Nov, 1931
Record Defeat: 2-11 v Sheffield U Jan, 1926
Most Capped Player: Alf Sherwood, Wales 39
Most League Appearances: Phil Dwyer, 471
Record Transfer Fee Received:
£500,000 for Simon Haworth, Jun 1997
Record Transfer Fee Paid:
£180,000 for Godfrey Ingram, Sept 1982
Capacity: 15,585   **Fanzine:** The Thin Blue Line
Away Capacity: 1,800 **Unofficial site:** www.cardiffcity.com
Disabled places: 16

Last 5 Seasons:	Last 5 Managers:
1997: Div 3 - 7th	Kenny Hibbitt (96-98)
1998: Div 3 - 21st	Frank Burrows (98-99)
1999: Div 3 - 3rd	Billy Ayre (99-00)
2000: Div 2 - 21st	Bobby Gould (00)
2001: Div 3 - 2nd	Alan Cork (00-Pre)

Cardiff City Football Club

Travel:

Rail: Park Halt (from Cardiff Central) 08457 484950

Bus: National Coach Enquiries 0870 6082608

Car:

From all Directions: Come off the M4 at junction 33. Follow the A4232 for six miles until you get to a roundabout. Take the second exit (still on the A423) and follow signposts for Cardiff. Stay in the left hand lane of the slip road and you will automatically join Leckwith Road. Follow this road to the traffic lights and upon reaching them turn right into Sloper Road. The ground is on the left hand side.

MY RATING

Date Visited: _____

Rating out of 10:

1 2 3 4 5 6 7 8 9 10

Note: _____

Honours:

Football League: Divison 1. Runners-up: 1923-1924. Division 2. Runners-up: 1920-1921, 1951-1952, 1959-1960. Division 3 (S). Champions: 1946-1947. Division 3. Champions: 1992-1993. Runners-up: 1975-1976, 1982-1983, 2000 -2001. Division 4. Runners-up: 1987-1988.

FA Cup: Winners: 1927. Runners-up: 1925.

Football League Cup: Semi-final 1966.

Welsh Cup: Winners 21 times. Charity Shield: Winners 1927.

European Competitions:

European Cup-Winners' Cup: 1964-1965, 1965-1966, 1967-1968 (semi-finalists), 1968-1969, 1969-1970, 1970-1971, 1971-1972, 1973-1974, 1974-1975, 1976-1977, 1977-1978, 1988-1989, 1991-1992, 1992-1993, 1993-1994.

Carlisle United Football Club

Address:
Brunton Park
Warwick Road
Carlisle, CA1 1LL
Switch Board: 01228 526237
Ticket Office: 01228 526237
Website:
www.carlisleunited.co.uk
Nickname: The Cumbrians
Year Formed: 1903
Record Attendance: 27,500 v Birmingham C Jan, 1957. v Middlesbrough Feb, 1970
Record Receipts: £146,000 v Tottenham H Sept, 1997
Record League Victory: 8-0 v Hartlepool U Sept, 1928. Scunthorpe United Dec, 1952
Record Cup Victory: 6-0 v Shepshed Dynamo Nov, 1996
Record Defeat: 1-11 v Hull C Jan, 1939
Most Capped Player: Eric Welsh, Northern Ireland 4
Most League Appearances: Allan Ross, 466
Record Transfer Fee Received:
£1,500,000 for Matt Jansen, Feb 1998
Record Transfer Fee Paid:
£121,000 for David Reeves, Dec 1993
Capacity: 16,651 **Fanzine:** Hit the Bar
Away Capacity: 1,900 **Unofficial site:** www.cufconline.org.uk
Disabled places: 40

Last 5 Seasons:	Last 5 Managers:
1997: Div 3 - 3rd	Mick Wadsworth (93-96)
1998: Div 2 - 23rd	Mervyn Day (96-97)
1999: Div 3 - 23rd	Michael Knighton (97-99)
2000: Div 3 - 23rd	Martin Wilkinson (99-00)
2001: Div 3 - 22nd	Ian Atkins (00-Pre)

Carlisle United Football Club

Travel:

Rail: Carlisle, 08457 484950

Bus: National Coach Enquiries 0870 6082608

Car:

From all Directions:

Exit the M6 at junction 43, Take the first turnoff at the roundabout, which is signposted for Carlisle City Centre. Follow the road through 2 sets of traffic lights, after you go through the second set the ground will come into view on the right hand side, just continue on this road until you arrive at the stadium.

Honours:

Football League: Division 1: Best season: 22nd, 1974-1975. Promoted from Division 2 (3rd) 1973-1974. Division 3. Champions: 1964-1965, 1994-1995. Runners-up: 1981-1982. Promoted from Division 3: 1996-1997. Division 4. Runners-up: 1963-1964.

FA Cup: Best season: 6th rd 1975.

Football League Cup: Semi-final 1970.

Auto Windscreens Shield: Winners: 1997. Runners-up: 1995.

MY RATING

Date Visited: _____

Rating out of 10:

1 2 3 4 5 6 7 8 9 10

Note: _____

Charlton Athletic Football Club

Address:
The Valley
Floyd Road
Charlton
London, SE7 8BL

Switch Board: 020 8333 4000

Ticket Office: 020 8333 4010

Website: www.cafc.co.uk

Nickname: The Addicks

Year Formed: 1905

Record Attendance: 75,031 v Aston Villa Feb, 1938

Record Receipts: £201,711 v QPR Jan, 2000

Record League Victory: 8-1 v Middlesbrough Sep, 1953

Record Cup Victory: 7-0 v Burton A Jan, 1956

Record Defeat: 1-11 v Aston Villa Nov, 1959

Most Capped Player: John Robinson, Wales 26

Most League Appearances: Sam Bartram, 583

Record Transfer Fee Received:
£4,370,000 for Danny Mills, Jun 1999

Record Transfer Fee Paid:
£4,750,000 for Jason Euell, Jul 2001

Capacity: 20,043 (26,500 - 2002) **Fanzine:** Goodbye Horse

Away Capacity: 2,600 **Unofficial site:** www.goodbyehorse.com

Disabled places: 70

Last 5 Seasons:	Last 5 Managers:
1997: Div 1 - 15th	Alan Mullery (81-82)
1998: Div 1 - 4th	Ken Craggs (82)
1999: Prem - 18th	Lennie Lawrence (82-91)
2000: Div 1 - 1st	S Gritt/A Curbishley (91-95)
2001: Prem - 9th	Alan Curbishley (95-Pre)

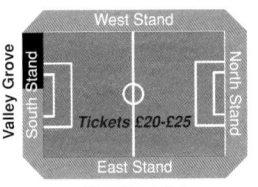

Charlton Athletic Football Club

Travel:

Rail: Charlton 08457 484950

Bus: National Coach Enquiries 0870 6082608

Car:

North, East, South:

Come off the M25 at junction 2 and head towards London on the A2 for 10 miles. Continue along the dual carriageway and the road becomes the A102 (M) Blackwall tunnel approach road. Leave at the junction after the A2 exit. Turn right (left for those coming through the tunnel) at the roundabout onto the A206 Woolwich Road. At the junction of Charlton Church Lane and Anchor and Hope Lane, you will see a major set of traffic lights go through these and then turn right at the second roundabout into Charlton Lane. Cross the railway crossing and then take the first right into Harvey gardens. Follow this road and you will arrive at the ground.

West:

Follow the A13 to the East India Dock Road and then take the A102 through the Blackwell Tunnel. Follow directions as if travelling North.

MY RATING

Date Visited: _____

Rating out of 10:
1 2 3 4 5 6 7 8 9 10

Note: _____

Charlton Athletic Football Club

Honours:

Football League: Division 1. Champions: 1999-2000. Runners-up: 1936-1937. Promoted from Division 1, 1997-1998 (play-offs). Division 2. Runners-up: 1935-1936, 1985-1986. Division 3 (S). Champions: 1928-1929, 1934-1935. Promoted from Division 3 (3rd) 1974-1975, 1980-1981.

FA Cup: Winners: 1947. Runners-up: 1946.

Football League Cup: Best season: 4th rd, 1963, 1966, 1979.

Full Members' Cup: Runners-up: 1987.

Chelsea Football Club

Address:
Stamford Bridge
Fulham Road
London, SW6 1HS
Switch Board: 020 7385 5545
Ticket Office: 020 7386 7799
Website: www.chelseafc.co.uk
Nickname: The Blues
Year Formed: 1905
Record Attendance: 82,905 v Arsenal Oct, 1935
Record Receipts: £488,960 v Liverpool Dec, 1995
Record League Victory: 9-2 v Glossop ME Sep, 1906
Record Cup Victory: 13-0 v Jeunesse Hautcharage Sep, 1971
Record Defeat: 1-8 v Wolverhampton W Sep, 1953
Most Capped Player: Dan Petrescu, Romania 43
Most League Appearances: Ron Harris, 655
Record Transfer Fee Received:
£4,500,000 for Michael Duberry, Jul 1999. Emerson, Aug 2000.
Record Transfer Fee Paid:
£15,000,000 for Jimmy Floyd Hasselbaink, Jun 2000
Capacity: 42,420 **Fanzine:** Matthew Harding's Blue & White Army
Away Capacity: 3,000 **Unofficial site:** www.chelsea-fc.org.uk
Disabled places: 40

Tickets £27-£33

Away Supporters

Last 5 Seasons:	Last 5 Managers:
1997: Prem - 6th	David Webb (93)
1998: Prem - 4th	Glenn Hoddle (93-96)
1999: Prem - 3rd	Ruud Gullit (96-98)
2000: Prem - 5th	Gianluca Vialli (98-00)
2001: Prem - 6th	Claudio Ranieri (00-Pre)

Chelsea Football Club

Travel:

Rail: Putney Bridge
08457 484950

Tube: Fulham Broadway
(District Line)

Bus: National Coach
Enquiries 0870 6082608

Car:

North, East or West:

Use the M25 to take you round to junction 15 and turn off onto the M4 towards London. Follow the M4 which becomes the A4 up to Hammersmith. Stay on the A4 over the Hammersmith flyover and for a further 1.5 miles before turning off for **Earls Court**. Go past Earls Court station and down the one way system until you hit Fulham Road, turn right at the traffic lights. Go straight on for 600 yards and the ground is on your right.

South:

Take junction 7 of the M25 and join the M23 which becomes the A23. Continue following the A23 until Streatham bearing left onto the A214. Follow the A214 passing Tooting Bec Tube station and continue along following signs for Wandsworth. At the large roudabout (with strange looking monument in the middle), go straight across and head for Wandsworth bridge to cross the river. Head straight up Wandsworth Bridge Road. At the junction with **New Kings Road** turn right and then immediately left. This will take you up to Fulham Broadway, turn right onto Fulham Road and the ground is 400 yards on your left.

MY RATING

Date Visited: _____

Rating out of 10:

1 2 3 4 5 6 7 8 9 10

Note: _____
_____
_____
_____

Chelsea Football Club

Honours:

Football League: Division 1. Champions: 1954-1955. Division 2. Champions. 1983-1984, 1988-1989. Runners-up: 1906-1907, 1911-1912, 1929-1930, 1962-1963, 1976-1977.

FA Cup: Winners: 1970, 1997, 2000. Runners-up: 1915, 1967, 1994.

Football League Cup: Winners: 1965, 1998. Runners-up: 1972.

Full Members' Cup: Winners: 1986.

Zenith Data Systems Cup: Winners: 1990.

European Competitions:

European Cup: 1999-2000.

European Fairs Cup: 1958-1960, 1965-1966, 1968-1969.

European Cup-Winners' Cup: 1970-1971 (winners), 1971-1972, 1994-1995, 1997-1998 (winners), 1998-1999 (semi-finals).

Super Cup: 1998-1999 (winners).

Cheltenham Town Football Club

Address:
Whaddon Road
Cheltenham
Gloucestershire
GL52 5NA

Switch Board: 01242 573558
Ticket Office: 01242 573558
Website: www.cheltenhamtownfc.com
Nickname: The Robins
Year Formed: 1892
Record Attendance: 8,326 v Reading Nov, 1956
Record Receipts: £40,000 v Yeovil T Apr, 1999
Record League Victory: 11-0 v Bourneville Ath Apr, 1933
Record Cup Victory: 12-0 v Chippenham R Nov, 1935
Record Defeat: 1-10 v Merthyr T Mar, 1952
Most Capped Player: Nil
Most League Appearances: Roger Thorndale, 523
Record Transfer Fee Received:
£60,000 for Christer Warren, 1995
Record Transfer Fee Paid:
£25,000 for Kim Casey, 1991
Capacity: 6,114   **Fanzine:** They've scored again
Away Capacity: 1,200
Unofficial site: www.thisengland.freeserve.co.uk
Disabled places: 6

Last 5 Seasons:	Last 5 Managers:
1997: Sth L - 2nd	Dave Lewis (90-91)
1998: Conf - 2nd	Ally Robertson (91-92)
1999: Conf - 1st	Lindsay Parsons (92-95)
2000: Div 3 - 8th	Chris Robinson (95-97)
2001: Div 3 - 9th	Steve Cotterill (97-Pre)

Cheltenham Town Football Club

Travel:

Rail: Cheltenham 08457 484950

Bus: National Coach Enquiries 0870 6082608

Car:
North:

Leave the M5 at junction 10 and take the A4019 towards Cheltenham. Keep straight on through the lights, until you come to a roundabout, at which you turn left. Continue up this road going over a double mini roundabout. Keep going for about 300 yards and then turn right into Swindon Lane. Go over the level crossing and straight over the next roundabout (signposted Prestbury). Turn right into Albert Road and at the roundabout turn left into Prestbury Road, continue and then turn right into Whaddon Road. The ground is down on the left.

South/West:

Leave the M5 at junction 11 turning right towards Cheltenham. Go across 1st roundabout, GCHQ is on your left. Turn left at the next roundabout, into Queen Elizabeth Way. Go straight over the next roundabout, until you come to a big roundabout, where you will see a McDonalds on the corner. Go straight across and continue up this road going over a double mini roundabout. Then as North.

East:

Take the A40 into Cheltenham. Continue to the set of traffic lights with Hales Road, turn right. After two miles, the road bends right and then left, directly after this, there is a left turn which is Whaddon Road. Go straight over at the next roundabout and continue driving until you reach the ground.

MY RATING

Date Visited: _____

Rating out of 10:

1 2 3 4 5 6 7 8 9 10

Note:
_____
_____
_____
_____

Cheltenham Town Football Club

Honours:

Football Conference: Champions: 1998-1999. Runners-up: 1997-1998.

FA Trophy: Winners: 1997-1998.

Southern League: Champions: 1984-1985.

Southern League Cup: Winners: 1957-1958. Runners-up: 1968-1969, 1984-1985. Southern League Merit Cup: Winners: 1984-1985. Southern League Championship Shield: Winners: 1985.

Gloucestershire Senior Cup: Winners: 1998-1999.

Gloucestershire Northern Senior Professional Cup: Winners 30 times.

Midland Floodlit Cup: Winners: 1985-1986, 1986-1987, 1987-1988.

Mid Gloucester League: Champions: 1896-1897.

Gloucester and District League: Champions: 1902-1903, 1905-1906.

Cheltenham League: Champions: 1910-1911, 1913-1914.

North Gloucestershire League: Champions: 1913-1914.

Gloucestershire Northern Senior League: Champions: 1928-1929, 1932-1933.

Gloucestershire Northern Senior Amateur Cup: Winners: 1929-1930, 1930-1931, 1932-1933, 1933-1934, 1934-1935.

Chesterfield Football Club

Address:
The Recreation Ground
Saltergate
Chesterfield
Derbyshire, S40 4SX
Switch Board: 01246 209765
Ticket Office: 01246 209765
Website: www.chesterfield-fc.co.uk
Nickname: The Spireites
Year Formed: 1866

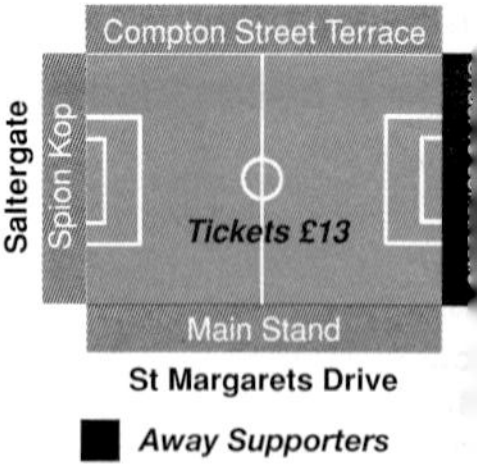

Record Attendance: 30,968 v Newcastle U Apr, 1939
Record Receipts: £45,000 v Mansfield T May, 1995
Record League Victory: 10-0 v Glossop NE Jan, 1903
Record Cup Victory: 5-0 v Wath Ath Nov, 1925
Record Defeat: 0-10 v Gillingham Sep, 1987
Most Capped Player: Walter McMillen/Mark Williams, Northern Ireland 4
Most League Appearances: Dave Blakey, 613
Record Transfer Fee Received:
£750,000 for Kevin Davies, May 1997
Record Transfer Fee Paid:
£250,000 for Jason Lee, Aug 1998
Capacity: 8,960   **Fanzine:** Tora Tora Tora
Away Capacity: 2,700 **Unofficial site:** www.cfcaspire.com
Disabled places: 30

Last 5 Seasons:	Last 5 Managers:
1997: Div 2 - 10th	Kevin Randall (87-88)
1998: Div 2 - 10th	Paul Hart (88-91)
1999: Div 2 - 9th	Chris McMenemy (91-93)
2000: Div 2 - 24th	John Duncan (93-00)
2001: Div 3 - 3rd	Nicky Law (00-Pre)

Chesterfield Football Club

Travel:

Rail: Chesterfield 08457 484950

Bus: National Coach Enquiries 0870 6082608

Car:

North: From the M1 come off at junction 30. Take the A619 from the roundabout and continue into Chesterfield town centre. Pick up signs for Old Brampton and then by following this road it will take you to Saltergate. The ground is on your right.

South: Follow the A61 into Chesterfield. Turn left at the roundabout with the A617 and then turn left again at the next roundabout. At the following roundabout take the fourth exit into Foljambe Road. At the end of this road is Saltergate and the ground is directly in front of you.

East: Take the A617 to Chesterfield town centre. Turn left at the roundabout with the A619, then travel as if going South.

West: Take the A619 into Chesterfield town centre. As you enter the town there is a crossroads with the A632; turn left into Old Hall Road and then right at the bottom into Saltergate. The ground is half a mile on your left.

Honours:

Football League: Division 2. Best season: 4th, 1946-1947. Division 3 (N). Champions: 1930-1931, 1935-1936. Runners-up: 1933-1934 Promoted 2000-2001. Division 4. Champions: 1969-1970, 1984-1985.

FA Cup: Semi-final: 1997. Football League Cup: Best season: 5th rd, 1965. Anglo-Scottish Cup: Winners: 1981.

MY RATING

Date Visited: _____

Rating out of 10:

1 2 3 4 5 6 7 8 9 10

Note: _____

Colchester United Football Club

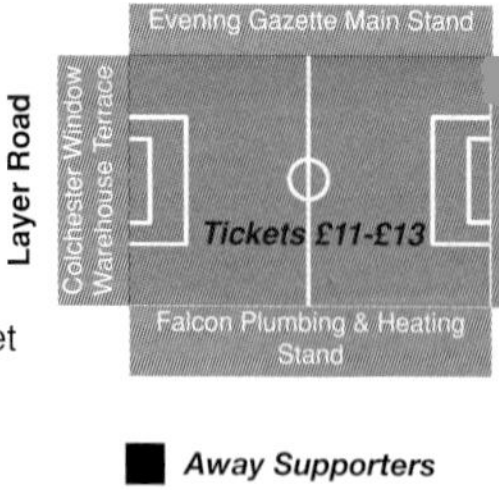

Address:
Layer Road
Colchester
Essex, CO2 7JJ
Switch Board: 01206 508800
Ticket Office: 01206 508800
Website: www.colchesterunited.net
Nickname: The U's
Year Formed: 1937
Record Attendance:
19,072 v Reading Nov, 1948
Record Receipts: £26,330 v Barrow May, 1992
Record League Victory: 9-1 v Bradford C Dec, 1961
Record Cup Victory: 7-1 v Yeovil T Dec, 1958
Record Defeat: 0-8 v Leyton Orient Oct, 1989
Most Capped Player: Nil
Most League Appearances: Micky Cook 613
Record Transfer Fee Received:
£2,250,000 for Lomano Lua-Lua, Sep 2000
Record Transfer Fee Paid:
£50,000 for Neil Gregory, Mar 1998
Capacity: 7,556   **Fanzine:** The Blue Eagle
Away Capacity: 1,400 **Unofficial site:** www.coluonline.com
Disabled places: 6

Last 5 Seasons:	Last 5 Managers:
1997: Div 3 - 8th	Roy McDonough (91-94)
1998: Div 3 - 4th	George Burley (94)
1999: Div 2 - 18th	Steve Wignall (95-99)
2000: Div 2 - 18th	Mick Wadsworth (99)
2001: Div 2 - 17th	Steve Whitton (99-Pre)

Colchester United Football Club

Travel:

Rail: Colchester Town 08457 484950

Bus: National Coach Enquiries 0870 6082608

Car:

North:

Travelling on the A12 to Colchester, do not take the first turn off but continue on the A12 towards London and take the Halstead/Cambridge turn off. At the top of the slip road turn left and continue along Essex Yeomanry Way then left at roundabout into London Road. Proceed for just over 3/4 mile to the traffic lights. Turn right at the lights and follow this road until you reach it's end where a pub (Leather Bottle) is on left. Turn left and follow this until you reach the traffic lights at Boadicea Way, where you turn right. Go to end of this road and turn left; this is Layer Rd and the ground is about 1/4 mile on left.

South:

Take the A12 towards Colchester town centre until you reach the roundabout with the A604. Take the third exit into Spring Lane and then continue along this road until you get to a T-junction. Turn right into Norman Way and go straight over the crossroads into Boadicea Way. At the bottom of Boadicea Way there is a T-junction. Turn left onto Layer Road and the ground is 250 Meters on your left.

MY RATING

Date Visited: _____

Rating out of 10:

1 2 3 4 5 6 7 8 9 10

Note: _____

Colchester United Football Club

Honours:

Football League: Promoted from Division 3. 1997-1998 (play-offs). Division 4. Runners-up: 1961-1962.

FA Cup: Best season: 6th rd, 1971.

Football League Cup: Best season: 5th rd, 1975.

Auto Windscreens Shield: Runners-up: 1997.

GM Vauxhall Conference: Winners: 1991-1992.

FA Trophy: Winners: 1992.

Coventry City Football Club

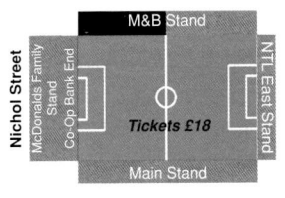

Address:
Highfield Road Stadium
King Richard Street
Coventry, CV2 4FW
Switch Board: 02476 234000
Ticket Office: 02476 234000
Website: www.ccfc.co.uk
Nickname: The Sky Blues
Year Formed: 1883
Record Attendance:
51,455 v Wolverhampton W Apr, 1967
Record Receipts:
£405,369 v Charlton Ath Jan, 2000
Record League Victory: 9-0 v Bristol C Apr, 1934
Record Cup Victory: 7-0 v Scunthorpe U Nov, 1934
Record Defeat: 2-10 v Norwich C Mar, 1930
Most Capped Player: Magnus Hedman, Sweden 31
Most League Appearances: Steve Ogrizovic, 507
Record Transfer Fee Received:
£12,500,000 for Robbie Keane, Jul 2000
Record Transfer Fee Paid:
£6,000,000 for Robbie Keane, Aug 1999
Capacity: 23,633   **Fanzine:** Twist and Shout
Away Capacity: 4,100 **Unofficial site:** www.sbs.depro.co.uk
Disabled places: Varies

Away Supporters

Last 5 Seasons:	Last 5 Managers:
1997: Prem - 17th	Bobby Gould (92-93)
1998: Prem - 11th	Phil Neal (93-95)
1999: Prem - 15th	Ron Atkinson (95-96)
2000: Prem - 14th	Gordon Strachan (96-01)
2001: Prem - 19th	Roland Nilsson (01 - Pre)

Coventry City Football Club

Travel:

Rail: Colchester Town
08457 484950

Bus: National Coach
Enquiries 0870 6082608

Car:

North:

Take the M1 to junction 21 and join the M69 continuing at junction 2 onto the A4600 following signs to the centre. This road becomes the Walsgrave Road which turns right into Swan Lane. The ground is ahead on the left.

South:

Take M40 to junction 15 onto A46. Continue on A46 which changes to A4114 for approx 10 miles. Then take A423 signposted city centre. After approximately 2 miles take A4600 signposted Leicester. Follow this road and turn left into Swan Lane. The Ground is on the left.

West/East:

Approaching on the M6 in either direction, turn off onto the A4600 at junction 2. Then as route for North.

MY RATING

Date Visited: _____

Rating out of 10:

1 2 3 4 5 6 7 8 9 10

Note: _____

Coventry City Football Club

Honours:

Football League: Division 1. Best season: 6th, 1969-1970. Division 2. Champions: 1966-1967. Division 3. Champions: 1963-1964. Division 3 (S). Champions: 1935-1936. Runners-up: 1933-1934. Division 4. Runners-up: 1958-1959.

FA Cup: Winners: 1987.

Football League Cup: Semi-final 1981, 1990.

European Competitions:

European Fairs Cup: 1970-1971.

Crewe Alexandra Football Club

Address:
Gresty Road
Crewe
Cheshire, CW2 6EB 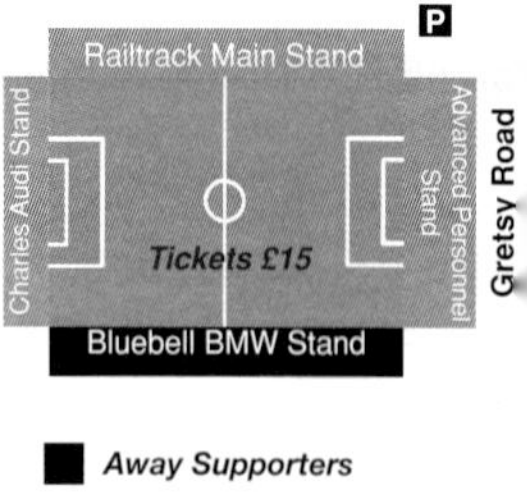
Switch Board: 01270 213014
Ticket Office: 01270 252610
Website: www.crewealex.net
Nickname: The Railwaymen
Year Formed: 1877
Record Attendance:
20,000 v Tottenham H Jan, 1960
Record Receipts: £41,093 v Liverpool Jan, 1992
Record League Victory: 8-0 v Rotherham U Oct, 1932
Record Cup Victory: 8-0 v Hartlepool U Oct, 1995
Record Defeat: 2-13 v Tottenham H Feb, 1960
Most Capped Player: Bill Lewis, Wales 9
Most League Appearances: Tommy Lowry, 436
Record Transfer Fee Received:
£3,000,000 for Seth Johnson, May 1999
Record Transfer Fee Paid:
£650,000 for Rodney Jack, Jun 1998
Capacity: 10,046   **Fanzine:** Super Darioland
Away Capacity: 1,680 **Unofficial site:** www.crewealex.co.uk
Disabled places: Varies

Last 5 Seasons:	Last 5 Managers:
1997: Div 2 - 6th	Warwick Rimmer (78-79)
1998: Div 1 - 11th	Tony Waddington (79-81)
1999: Div 1 - 18th	Arfon Griffiths (81-82)
2000: Div 1 - 19th	Peter Morris (82-83)
2001: Div 1 - 14th	Dario Gradi (83-Pre)

Crewe Alexandra Football Club

Travel:

Rail: Crewe 08457 484950

Bus: National Coach Enquiries 0870 6082608

Car: North:

Exit M6 at junction 17 (A534). At the T-junction turn right for Crewe and follow A534 (signposted Crewe / Nantwich). After about six miles, at the third roundabout, travel for a further mile and you will pass the Crewe Arms on your right and Crewe Station on your left. Gresty Road is the first left after the Station. Beware: on match days, you may not be able to take this left turn, and may be redirected to the next left (100 yards, South St, at traffic lights).

South / East: Exit the M6 at junction 16 (A500). At the roundabout follow signs for Crewe. After about two miles, turn right at the roundabout (A5020) towards Crewe then left at the next roundabout (three quarters of a mile). Go straight on at the next roundabout (Rookery pub on right), passing the Brocklebank pub on the left; then left at the next roundabout, taking you into Nantwich Road, passing the Crewe Arms Hotel on your right and Crewe Station on your left. Then as North.

West: From Nantwich, follow Crewe Road, A534 (signs to Crewe Station, 4 miles), which will eventually bring you along Nantwich Road.

MY RATING

Date Visited: _____

Rating out of 10:
1 2 3 4 5 6 7 8 9 10

Note: _____

Crewe Alexandra Football Club

Honours:

Football League: Promoted from Division 2. 1996-1997 (play-offs).

FA Cup: Semi-final 1888.

Football League Cup: Best season: 3rd rd, 1975, 1976, 1979, 1993, 1999, 2000.

Welsh Cup: Winners: 1936, 1937.

Crystal Palace Football Club

Address:
Selhurst Park
London
SE25 6PU
Switch Board: 020 8768 6000
Ticket Office: 020 8771 8841
Website: www.cpfc.co.uk
Nickname: The Eagles
Year Formed: 1861
Record Attendance: 51,482 v Burnley May, 1979
Record Receipts: £327,124 v Manchester U Apr, 1993
Record League Victory: 9-0 v Barrow Oct, 1959
Record Cup Victory: 8-0 v Southend U Sept, 1989
Record Defeat: 0-9 v Burnley Feb, 1909. v Liverpool Sept, 1990
Most Capped Player: Eric Young, Wales 19
Most League Appearances: Jim Cannon 571
Record Transfer Fee Received:
£4,500,000 for Chris Armstrong, Jun 1995
Record Transfer Fee Paid:
£2,750,000 for Valerien Ismael, Jan 1998
Capacity: 26,400 **Fanzine:** One More Point
Away Capacity: 2,500-9000
Unofficial site: www.holmesdale.net
Disabled places: 28

Last 5 Seasons:	Last 5 Managers:
1997: Div 1 - 6th	Attilio Lombardo (98)
1998: Prem - 20th	Terry Venables (98-99)
1999: Div 1 - 14th	Steve Coppell (99-00)
2000: Div 1 - 15th	Alan Smith (00-01)
2001: Div 1 - 21st	Steve Bruce (01-Pre)

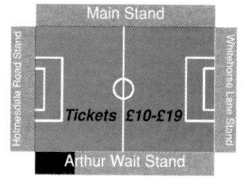

Crystal Palace Football Club

Travel:

Rail: Norwood Junction, Thornton Heath, Selhurst 08457 484950

Bus: National Coach Enquiries 0870 6082608

Car:

North: **From M1, take the A406 North Circular Road (WestBound) to Chiswick Roundabout.** Take the third exit at the roundabout onto Chiswick High Road, then first left onto the A205 (signposted Kew). After two miles you reach a T-junction at which you should turn left (signposted Putney). Continue until the road merges with the A3, then a mile later turn right onto the A214. Once in Streatham turn right onto the A23. After 1 mile turn left onto Green Lane (B273) and at end turn left into High Street which runs into Whitehorse Lane. Selhurst Park is on your right.

East: From M25, take junction 4 which becomes the A21 and then A232. Follow the A232 (signposted Croydon) to Shirley then join A215 (signposted Norwood). In 2.2 miles turn left B266 into Whitehorse Lane.

South: From the M25, take junction 8 and take the A23, following the signs for Thornton Heath. Turn right onto the A235. Once on the A235 turn immediately left onto the B266 Brigstock Road which becomes the High Street, then travel as if going North.

West: Take the M4 to Chiswick, then travel as if going North.

MY RATING

Date Visited: _____

Rating out of 10:

1 2 3 4 5 6 7 8 9 10

Note: _____

Crystal Palace Football Club

Honours:

Football League: Division 1. Champions 1993-1994. Promoted from Division 1, 1996-1997 (play-offs). Division 2. Champions 1978-1979. Runners-up: 1968-1969. Division 3. Runners-up: 1963-1964; Division 3 (S) - Champions 1920-1921; Runners-up: 1928-1929, 1930-1931, 1938-1939; Division 4. Runners-up: 1960-1961.

FA Cup: Runners-up: 1990.

Football League Cup: Semi-final: 1993, 1995, 2001.

Zenith Data Systems Cup: Winners: 1991.

Darlington Football Club

Address:
Feethams Ground
Darlington
DL1 5JB
Switch Board: 01325 240240
Ticket Office: 01325 240500
Website: www.darlington-fc.net
Nickname: The Quakers
Year Formed: 1883
Record Attendance: 21,023 v Bolton Nov, 1960
Record Receipts: £32,300 v Rochdale May, 1991
Record League Victory: 9-2 v Lincoln C Jan, 1928
Record Cup Victory: 7-2 v Evenwood T Nov, 1956
Record Defeat: 0-10 v Doncaster R Jan, 1964
Most Capped Player: Jason Devos, Canada 3
Most League Appearances: Ron Greener, 442
Record Transfer Fee Received:
£400,000 for Jason Devos, Oct 1998
Record Transfer Fee Paid:
£95,000 for Nick Cusack, Jan 1992
Capacity: 8,500 **Fanzine:** Where's the Money Gone?
Away Capacity: 700 **Unofficial site:** www.wtmg.assets.org.uk
Disabled places: 24

Last 5 Seasons:	Last 5 Managers:
1997: Div 3 - 18th	Alan Murray (93-95)
1998: Div 3 - 19th	Paul Futcher (95)
1999: Div 3 - 11th	Jim Platt (95-96)
2000: Div 3 - 4th	David Hodgson (96-00)
2001: Div 3 - 20th	Gary Bennett (00-Pre)

Darlington Football Club

Travel:

Rail: Darlington 08457 484950

Bus: National Coach Enquiries 0870 6082608

Car:

At the time of writing, Darlington are due to relocate to a new ground who's name has not yet been decided. The move will occur in line with the start of the 2002 / 2003 season.

MY RATING

Date Visited: _____

Rating out of 10:
1 2 3 4 5 6 7 8 9 10

Note: _____

Directions for Feethams:

North:

Use the A1M then A167 (signposted Darlington) into the town centre. Follow signs for Northallerton into Victoria Road (part of the ring road). Darlington FC is on the left immediately after Feethams roundabout below Safeways.

South:

Use the A1M and A66M then A66. Follow signs to Darlington Town Centre. Take the fourth exit at the first major roundabout into Victoria Road and then turn into Feethams.

East/West:

Use the A66 or A67 and then B6280 (signposted Darlington) into town centre, then follow signs for Northallerton into Victoria Road. Feethams is on the left immediately after Feethams roundabout.

Darlington Football Club

Honours:

Football League: Division 2. Best season: 15th, 1925-1926.
Division 3 (N). Champions: 1924-1925. Runners-up: 1921-1922.
Division 4. Champions: 1990-1991. Runners-up: 1965-1966.

FA Cup: Best season: 5th rd, 1958.

Football League Cup: Best season: 5th rd, 1968.

GM Vauxhall Conference: Champions: 1989-1990.

Derby Football Club

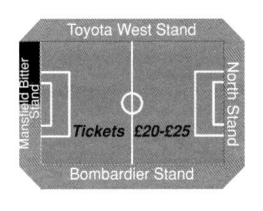

Address:
Pride Park Stadium
Derby
DE24 8XL
Switch Board: 01332 202202
Ticket Office: 01332 209999
Website: www.dcfc.co.uk
Nickname: The Rams
Year Formed: 1884

Away Supporters

Record Attendance: 41,826 v Tottenham H Sep, 1969
Record Receipts: £425,804 v Huddersfield T Feb, 1999
Record League Victory: 9-0 v Wolverhampton W Jan, 1891
Record Cup Victory: 12-0 v Finn Harps Sept, 1976
Record Defeat: 2-11 v Everton, 1889
Most Capped Player: Deon Burton, Jamaica 35
Most League Appearances: Kevin Hector, 486
Record Transfer Fee Received:
£5,300,000 for Christian Dailly, Aug 1998
Record Transfer Fee Paid:
£3,000,000 to £4,000,000 for Lee Morris, Oct 1999
Capacity: 33,597   **Fanzine:** None at present
Away Capacity: 5,000 **Unofficial site:** www.ramzone.co.uk
Disabled places: 70

Last 5 Seasons:	Last 5 Managers:
1997: Prem - 12th	Peter Taylor (82-84)
1998: Prem - 9th	Roy McFarland (84)
1999: Prem - 8th	Arthur Cox (84-93)
2000: Prem - 16th	Roy McFarland (93-95)
2001: Prem - 17th	Jim Smith (95-Pre)

Derby County Football Club

Travel:

Rail: Derby Midland
08457 484950

Bus: National Coach
Enquiries 0870 6082608

Car:

North:

Leave the M1 at junction 28 and follow A38 into Derby. Follow signs for A52 (Nottingham) off the Pentagon Island in Derby. After 1 mile, look for a large Toys R Us store on the right. Take first left at signs for the Wyvern Shopping Centre (also signposted Pride Park Stadium) and continue to the traffic island. Take the second exit, passing Sainsbury's on your right, and continue to the next traffic island. Take the first exit over bridge into **Pride Park**. The stadium is on the left.

South:

Leave the M1 at junction 25. At the roundabout take the first left signposted Derby (A52). Stay on this road for 5 miles, following signs for the city centre. Look out for signs for the Travel Inn on your left and a signpost for Pride Park Stadium. Take next left into the Wyvern Shopping Centre and continue to the traffic island. Take first exit over bridge into Pride Park. The stadium is on the left.

MY RATING

Date Visited: _____

Rating out of 10:

1 2 3 4 5 6 7 8 9 10

Note: _____

Derby County Football Club

Honours:

Football League: Division 1. Champions: 1971-1972, 1974-1975. Runners-up: 1895-1896, 1929-1930, 1935-1936, 1995-1996. Division 2. Champions: 1911-1912, 1914-1915, 1968-1969, 1986-1987. Runners-up: 1925-1926. Division 3 (N). Champions: 1956-1957. Runners-up: 1955-1956.

FA Cup: Winners: 1946. Runners-up: 1898, 1899, 1903.

Football League Cup: Semi-final: 1968.

Texaco Cup: Winners: 1972.

European Competitions:

European Cup: 1972-1973, 1975-1976.

UEFA Cup: 1974-1975, 1976-1977.

Anglo-Italian Cup: Runners-up: 1993.

Everton Football Club

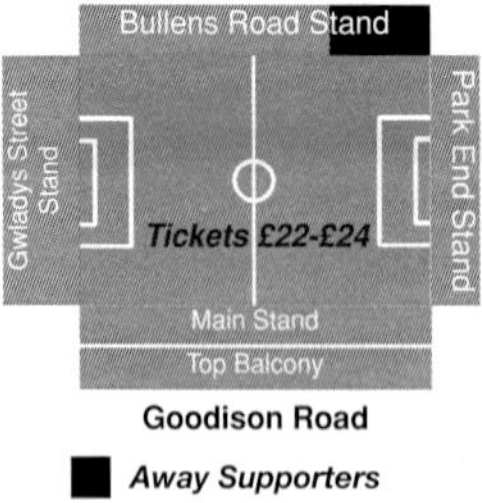

Address:
Goodison Park
Goodison Road
Liverpool, L4 4EL
Switch Board: 0151 330 2200
Ticket Office: 0151 330 2200
Website: www.evertonfc.com
Nickname: The Toffees
Year Formed: 1878
Record Attendance: 78,299 v Liverpool Sept, 1948
Record Receipts: £730,000 v Manchester U Sept, 2000
Record League Victory: 9-1 v Manchester C Sept, 1906
Record Cup Victory: 11-2 v Derby Co Jan, 1890
Record Defeat: 4-10 v Tottenham H Oct, 1958
Most Capped Player: Neville Southall, 92 Wales
Most League Appearances: Neville Southall, 578
Record Transfer Fee Received:
£10,000,000 for Francis Jeffers, Jun 2001
Record Transfer Fee Paid:
£5,750,000 for Nick Barmby, Oct 1996
Capacity: 40,170   **Fanzine:** When the Skies are Grey
Away Capacity: 3,000 **Unofficial site:** www.everton-mad.co.uk
Disabled places: 54

Last 5 Seasons:	Last 5 Managers:
1997: Prem - 15th	Howard Kendall (90-93)
1998: Prem - 17th	Mike Walker (94)
1999: Prem - 14th	Joe Royle (94-97)
2000: Prem - 13th	Howard Kendall (97-98)
2001: Prem - 16th	Walter Smith (98-Pre)

Everton Football Club

Travel:

Rail: Kirkdale 08457 484950

Bus: National Coach Enquiries 0870 6082608

Car:

North:

Approaching on the M6, exit at junction 26 onto the M58 and continue until the end. At junction 7 turn left onto the A59 (Ormskirk Road). Continue on this road which becomes Rice Lane, and cross over the roundabout into County Road. After 1/4 mile turn left into Everton Valley and then Walton Lane. Goodison Road and the ground are on the left.

South:

Approaching on the M6, exit at junction 21a onto the M62. Exit the M62 at junction 4 and get onto the A5080. At the junction with the A5058 turn right and continue along this road as it becomes Queens Drive. Continue to the junction with Walton Hall Avenue and turn left onto the A580 Walton Lane. Goodison Road and the ground are on the right.

East:

Approaching on the M62, exit at junction 4 and get onto the A5058. Then travel as if going South.

MY RATING

Date Visited: _____

Rating out of 10:
1 2 3 4 5 6 7 8 9 10

Note: _____

Everton Football Club

Honours:

Football League: Division 1. Champions: 1890-1891, 1914-1915, 1927-1928, 1931-1932, 1938-1939, 1962-1963, 1969-1970, 1984-1985, 1986-1987. Runners-up: 1889-1890, 1894-1895, 1901-1902, 1904-1905, 1908-1909, 1911-1912, 1985-1986. Division 2. Champions: 1930-1931. Runners-up: 1953-1954.

FA Cup: Winners: 1906, 1933, 1966, 1984, 1995. Runners-up: 1893, 1897, 1907, 1968, 1985, 1986, 1989.

Football League Cup: Runners-up: 1977, 1984.

League Super Cup: Runners-up: 1986.

Simod Cup: Runners-up: 1989.

Zenith Data Systems Cup: Runners-up: 1991.

European Competitions:

European Cup: 1963-1964, 1970-1971.

European Cup-Winners' Cup: 1966-1967, 1984-1985 (winners), 1995-1996.

European Fairs Cup: 1962-1963, 1964-1965, 1965-1966.

UEFA Cup: 1975-1976, 1978-1979, 1979-1980.

Exeter Football Club

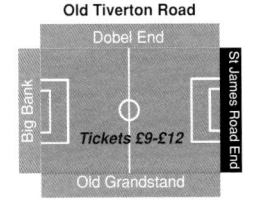

Address:
St James Park
Exeter
Devon, EX4 6PX
Switch Board: 01392 254073
Ticket Office: 01392 254073
Website: www.exetercityfc.co.uk
Nickname: The Grecians
Year Formed: 1904
Record Attendance: 20,984 v Sunderland Mar, 1931
Record Receipts: £59,862.98 v Aston Villa, Jan, 1994
Record League Victory: 8-1 v Coventry C Dec, 1926
Record Cup Victory: 14-0 v Weymouth Oct, 1908
Record Defeat: 0-9 v Notts Co Oct, 1948
Most Capped Player: Dermot Curtis, Eire 1
Most League Appearances: Arnold Mitchell, 495
Record Transfer Fee Received:
£500,000 for Martin Phillips, Nov 1995
Record Transfer Fee Paid:
£65,000 for Tony Kellow, Mar 1980
Capacity: 9,036   **Fanzine:** DNA
Away Capacity: 1,600 **Unofficial site:** www.ecfc.co.uk
Disabled places: 15

Last 5 Seasons:	Last 5 Managers:
1997: Div 3 - 22nd	Alan Ball (91-94)
1998: Div 3 - 15th	Terry Cooper (94-95)
1999: Div 3 - 12th	Peter Fox (95-00)
2000: Div 3 - 21st	Noel Blake (00-01)
2001: Div 3 - 19th	John Cornforth (01-Pre)

Exeter City Football Club

Travel:

Rail: Saint James' Park
08457 484950

Bus: National Coach
Enquiries 0870 6082608

Car: North: Take the M5 to junction 30. Follow the signs to Exeter City Centre, this will bring you onto Sidmouth Road which later becomes Heavitree Road. At the roundabout take the fourth exit onto Western Way. At the next roundabout take the second exit onto Old Tiverton Road, then left into St James Road. The ground is 75 Meters further down the road.

East: Follow the A30 into Exeter, you will join Heavitree Road, then travel as if going North.

South: Take the A38 into Exeter, following the city centre signs until you hit Western Way, then travel as if going North.

West: Take the A30 to A377. Follow the signs to the City Centre until you pick up Western Way, then as North.

Honours:

Football League: Division 3. Best season: 8th, 1979-1980. Division 3 (S). Runners-up: 1932-1933. Division 4. Champions: 1989-1990. Runners-up: 1976-1977.

FA Cup: Best season: 6th rd replay, 1931, 6th rd, 1981. Division 3 (S) Cup: Winners: 1934.

MY RATING

Date Visited: _____

Rating out of 10:
1 2 3 4 5 6 7 8 9 10

Note: _____

Fulham Football Club

Address:
Craven Cottage
Stevenage Road
Fulham
London, SW6 6HH

Switch Board: 020 7893 8383
Ticket Office: 020 7884 4710
Website: www.fulhamfc.co.uk
Nickname: The Cottagers
Year Formed: 1879
Record Attendance: 49,335 v Millwall Oct, 1938
Record Receipts: £139,235 v Watford May, 1998
Record League Victory: 10-1 v Ipswich T Dec, 1963
Record Cup Victory: 7-0 v Swansea C Nov, 1995
Record Defeat: 0-10 v Liverpool Sept, 1986
Most Capped Player: Johnny Haynes, England 56
Most League Appearances: Johnny Haynes, 594
Record Transfer Fee Received:
£2,250,000 for Geoff Horsfield, Jul 2000
Record Transfer Fee Paid:
£11,500,000 for Steve Marlet, Sept 2001
Capacity: 20,787 **Fanzine:** There's only one F in Fulham
Away Capacity: 1,500 **Unofficial site:** www.toofif.com
Disabled places: 21

Tickets £16-£20

Away Supporters

Last 5 Seasons:	Last 5 Managers:
1997: Div 3 - 2nd	Micky Adams (96-97)
1998: Div 2 - 6th	Ray Wilkins (97-98)
1999: Div 2 - 1st	Kevin Keegan (98-99)
2000: Div 1 - 9th	Paul Bracewell (99-00)
2001: Div 1 - 1st	Jean Tigana (00-Pre)

Fulham Football Club

Travel:

Rail: Putney Bridge
08457 484950

Tube: Putney Bridge
(District Line)

Bus: National Coach
Enquiries 0870 6082608

Car:

North:

Exit the M25 at junction 15 onto the M4 Eastbound. Remain on the M4, which becomes the A4, following signs to central London for 10.4 miles to the Hogarth roundabout. Here, take the second exit remain on the A4, passing the Griffin (Fullers) Brewery. At the Hammersmith flyover junction after 1.1 miles keep in left hand lane and exit the A4 (signposted Hammersmith, A306, A313, A219). Follow signs to Oxford (A40) for 0.3 miles to T-junction in front of Hayes accountants personnel. This is the Hammersmith roundabout. Continue round roundabout for 0.3 miles to where road runs underneath and parallel to the A4 and turn left into Fulham Palace Road.

Go straight on for 1.3 miles, and turn right into Bishops Park Road, which leads round to the ground.

South:

Leave the M25 at junction 10 and take the A3 towards Central London. After around eight miles, leave the A3 at the turn off for the A219. Take the A219 towards Putney. Continue straight on this road, down Putney High Street and across Putney Bridge.

MY RATING

Date Visited: _____

Rating out of 10:

1 2 3 4 5 6 7 8 9 10

Note: _____

Fulham Football Club

Over Putney Bridge, and after 0.1 miles go straight on at the junction / lights by the Pharoah & Firkin pub at mini roundabout after 0.1 miles by the Kings Head pub, go straight on into Fulham Palace Road. Ground is 0.2 miles on the left hand side.

Honours:
Football League: Division 1. Champions 2000-2001. Division 2. Champions: 1948-1949, 1998-1999. Runners-up: 1958-1959. Division 3 (S). Champions: 1931-1932. Division 3. Runners-up: 1970-1971, 1996-1997.

FA Cup: Runners-up: 1975.

Football League Cup: Best season: 5th rd, 1968, 1971, 2000.

Gillingham Football Club

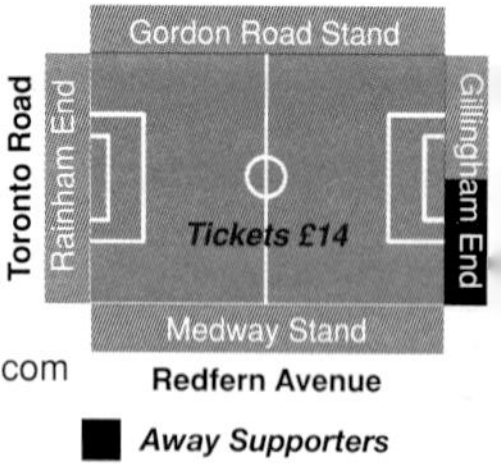

Address:
Priestfield Stadium
Redfern Avenue
Gillingham
Kent, ME7 4DD
Switch Board: 01634 300000
Ticket Office: 01634 300000
Website: www.gillinghamfootballclub.com
Nickname: The Gills
Year Formed: 1893
Record Attendance: 23,002 v QPR Jan, 1995
Record Receipts: £80,184 v Sheffield W Jan, 1995
Record League Victory: 10-0 v Chesterfield Sept, 1987
Record Cup Victory: 10-1 v Gorleston Nov, 1957
Record Defeat: 2-9 v Nottingham F Nov, 1950
Most Capped Player: Tony Cascarino, Republic of Ireland 3
Most League Appearances: John Simpson, 571
Record Transfer Fee Received:
£1,500,000 for Robert Taylor, Nov 1999
Record Transfer Fee Paid:
£600,000 for Carl Asaba, Aug 1998
Capacity: 10,600   Fanzine: Brian Moore's Head Looks Like
                            The London Planetarium
Away Capacity: 1,150 Disabled places: 56
Unofficial site: www.ourworld.compuserve.com/homepages/gillsf.c

Last 5 Seasons:	Last 5 Managers:
1997: Div 2 - 11th	Mike Flanagan (93-95)
1998: Div 2 - 8th	Neil Smillie (95)
1999: Div 2 - 4th	Tony Pulis (95-99)
2000: Div 2 - 3rd	Peter Taylor (99-00)
2001: Div 1 - 13th	Andy Hessenthaler (00-Pre)

Gillingham Football Club

Travel:

Rail: Gillingham 08457 484850

Bus: National Coach Enquiries 0870 6082608

Car:

From all Directions:

Leave the A2 at junction 4 and take the A278 signposted for Gillingham. At the third roundabout turn left onto the A2 towards Gillingham town centre. After a mile and a half you will come to a junction with the A231. Turn right into Nelson Road (A231). After the Bus station turn right into the Gillingham Road and the ground is down on your right.

MY RATING

Date Visited: _____

Rating out of 10:
1 2 3 4 5 6 7 8 9 10

Note: _____

Honours:

Football League: Promoted from Division 2. 1999-2000 (play-offs). Division 3. Runners-up: 1995-1996. Division 4. Champions: 1963-1964. Runners-up: 1973-1974.

FA Cup: Best season: 6th rd, 2000.

Football League Cup: Best season, 4th rd, 1964, 1997.

Grimsby Town Football Club

Address:
Blundell Park
Cleethorpes
North East Lincs
DN35 7PY

Switch Board: 01472 605050
Ticket Office: 01472 605050
Website: www.gtfc.co.uk
Nickname: The Mariners
Year Formed: 1878
Record Attendance: 31,657 v Wolverhampton W Feb, 1937
Record Receipts: £119,799 v Aston Villa Jan, 1994
Record League Victory: 9-2 v Darwen Apr, 1899
Record Cup Victory: 8-0 v Darlington Nov, 1885
Record Defeat: 1-9 v Arsenal Jan, 1931
Most Capped Player: Pat Glover, Wales 7
Most League Appearances: Keith Jobling, 448
Record Transfer Fee Received:
£1,500,000 for John Oster, Jul 1997
Record Transfer Fee Paid:
£400,000 for Lee Ashcroft, Aug 1998
Capacity: 10,033   **Fanzine:** Sing When We're Fishing
Away Capacity: 2,200 **Unofficial site:** www.grimsbytown.rivals.net
Disabled places: 88

Last 5 Seasons:	Last 5 Managers:
1997: Div 1 - 22nd	Alan Buckley (88-94)
1998: Div 2 - 3rd	Brian Laws (94-96)
1999: Div 1 - 11th	Kenny Swain (97)
2000: Div 1 - 20th	Alan Buckley (97-00)
2001: Div 1 - 18th	Lennie Lawrence (00-Pre)

Grimsby Town Football Club

Travel:

Rail: Cleethorpes 08457 484950

Bus: National Coach Enquiries 0870 6082608

Car:

North/West/SouthWest:

Head towards Grimsby on the M180 and stay on it when it becomes the A180. Follow the signs to Grimsby and Cleethorpes. Go straight over the next two rounabouts, at the third roundabout take the second exit. Continue past a railway and you will then join the A1098. As you continue along the A1098 it will become the Grimsby Road. Keep driving and you will see the ground.

South East:

Follow the A46 looking for signposts for Grimsby Town Centre. At the Roundabout turn left (signposted Grimsby) to the Grimsby Road and follow this road until you see the ground on your right.

MY RATING

Date Visited: _____

Rating out of 10:

1 2 3 4 5 6 7 8 9 10

Note: _____

Grimsby Town Football Club

Honours:

Football League: Division 1: Best season: 5th, 1934-1935. Division 2. Champions: 1900-1901, 1933-1934. Runners-up: 1928-1929. Promoted from Division 2. 1997-1998 (play-offs). Division 3 (N). Champions: 1925-1926, 1955-1956. Runners-up: 1951-1952. Division 3. Champions: 1979-1980. Runners-up: 1961-1962. Division 4. Champions: 1971-1972. Runners-up: 1978-1979, 1989-1990.

FA Cup: Semi-finals: 1936, 1939.

Football League Cup: Best season: 5th rd, 1980, 1985.

League Group Cup: Winners: 1982.

Auto Windscreen Shield: Winners: 1998.

Halifax Town Football Club

Address:
The Shay
Halifax
West Yorkshire, HX1 2YS
Switch Board: 01422 345543
Ticket Office: 01422 345543
Website: www.halifaxafc.co.uk
Nickname: The Shaymen
Year Formed: 1911

Skircoat Road
Skircoat Stand
South Terrace | North Stand
Tickets £10-£11
Under Re-Construction
Shaw Hill

■ *Away Supporters*

Record Attendance: 36,885 v Tottenham H Feb, 1953
Record Receipts: £36,267 v Bradford C Sep, 1998
Record League Victory: 6-0 v Bradford PA Dec, 1955
Record Cup Victory: 7-0 v Bishop Auckland Jan, 1967
Record Defeat: 0-13 v Stockport Co Jan, 1934
Most Capped Player: Nil
Most League Appearances: John Pickering, 367
Record Transfer Fee Received:
£350,000 for Geoff Horsfield, Oct 1998
Record Transfer Fee Paid:
£150,000 for Chris Tate, Jul 1999
Capacity: 14,000   Fanzine: Shayven Haven
Away Capacity: Varies
Unofficial site: www.shaymen.com
Disabled places: 36

Last 5 Seasons:	Last 5 Managers:
1997: Conf - 19th	George Mulhall (96-98)
1998: Conf - 1st	Kieran O'Regan (98-99)
1999: Div 3 - 10th	Mark Lillis (99-00)
2000: Div 3 - 18th	Paul Bracewell (00-01)
2001: Div 3 - 23rd	Parks/Redfearn(01 - Pre)

Halifax Town Football Club

Travel:

Rail: Halifax 08457 484950

Bus: National Coach Enquiries 0870 6082608

Car:

South, East, West: Travel towards the M62 (usually from M60 or M1). Follow signs for Leeds, Manchester, until such a time as Halifax is signposted. Leave at junction 24. On leaving the motorway, take the A629 towards Halifax. Go past the hospital and after half a mile turn right into Shaw Hill. The Shay is 200 Meters on your left.

North: Following the A629 go through Halifax until the road becomes Skircoat Road. Turn left onto Hunger Road and then right for Shaw Hill.

Honours:

Football League: Division 3: Best season: 3rd, 1970-1971.
Division 3 (N). Runners-up: 1934-1935. Division 4: Runners-up: 1968-1969.
FA Cup: Best season: 5th rd, 1933, 1953.
Football League Cup: Best season: 4th rd, 1964.
Vauxhall Conference: Champions: 1997-1998.

MY RATING

Date Visited: _____

Rating out of 10:
1 2 3 4 5 6 7 8 9 10

Note: _____

Hartlepool Football Club

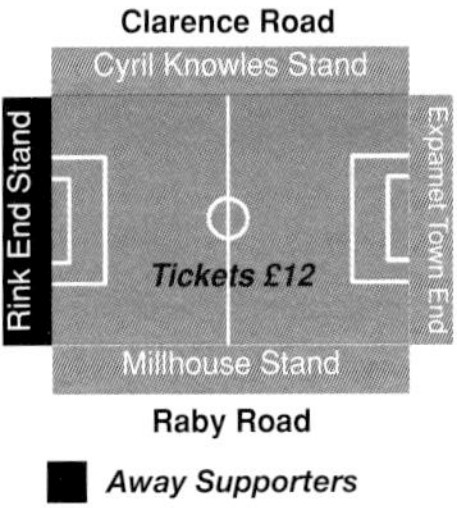

Address:
Victoria Park
Clarence Road
Hartlepool
TS24 8BZ
Switch Board: 01429 272584
Ticket Office: 01429 272584
Website: www.hartlepoolunited.co.uk
Nickname: The Pool
Year Formed: 1908
Record Attendance: 17,426 v Manchester U Jan, 1957
Record Receipts: £42,300 v Tottenham Hotspur Oct, 1990
Record League Victory: 10-1 v Barrow Apr, 1959
Record Cup Victory: 6-0 v North Shield Nov, 1946
Record Defeat: 1-10 v Wrexham Mar, 1962
Most Capped Player: Ambrose Fogarty, Republic of Ireland 1
Most League Appearances: Wattie Moore, 447
Record Transfer Fee Received:
£800,000 for Tommy Miller, Jul 2001
Record Transfer Fee Paid:
£60,000 for Andy Saville, Mar 1992
Capacity: 7,229   **Fanzine:** Monkey Business
Away Capacity: 760   **Unofficial site:** www.bizz.hufc.net
Disabled places: 12

Clarence Road
Cyril Knowles Stand
Rink End Stand
Expamet Town End
Tickets £12
Millhouse Stand
Raby Road

■ *Away Supporters*

Last 5 Seasons:	Last 5 Managers:
1997: Div 3 - 20th	John MacPhail (93-94)
1998: Div 3 - 17th	David McCreery (94-95)
1999: Div 3 - 22nd	Keith Houchen (95-96)
2000: Div 3 - 7th	Mick Tait (96-99)
2001: Div 3 - 4th	Chris Turner (99-Pre)

Hartlepool Football Club

Travel:

Rail: Hartlepool Church Street 08457 484950

Bus: National Coach Enquiries 0870 6082608

Car:

North:

Follow the A19 until you reach the A179 turn left, (signposted Hartlepool). This road (Hart Road) goes directly into the town centre. When you reach a crossroads, turn right down Raby Road and then take a left turn into Museum Road. Go left down Clarence Road, left again and the ground is in front of you.

South/West:

Approach via the A689 from the South & West. Follow this into the centre past the Middleton Grange Shopping Centre and then turn left onto the A179 Clarence Road and the ground is on your left.

Honours:

Football League: Division 3 (N). Runners-up: 1956-1957.

FA Cup: Best season: 4th rd, 1955, 1978, 1989, 1993.

Football League Cup: Best season: 4th rd, 1975.

MY RATING

Date Visited: _____

Rating out of 10:
1 2 3 4 5 6 7 8 9 10

Note: _____

Huddersfield Football Club

Address:
The Alfred McAlpine Stadium
Huddersfield
HD1 6PX
Switch Board: 01484 484100
Ticket Office: 01484 484123
Website: www.htafc.com
Nickname: The Terriers
Year Formed: 1908
Record Attendance: 67,037 v Arsenal Feb, 1932 (Leeds Road)
23,678 v Liverpool Dec, 1999 (Alfred McAlpine)
Record Receipts: £243,081 v Liverpool Dec, 1999
Record League Victory: 10-1 v Blackpool Dec, 1930
Record Cup Victory: 7-0 v Lincoln U Nov, 1991
Record Defeat: 1-10 v Manchester C Nov, 1987
Most Capped Player: Jimmy Nicholson, Northern Ireland 31
Most League Appearances: Billy Smith, 520
Record Transfer Fee Received:
£2,700,000 for Andy Booth, Jul 1996
Record Transfer Fee Paid:
£1,200,000 for Marcus Stewart, Jul 1996
Capacity: 24,500 **Fanzine:** Hanging on the Telephone
Away Capacity: 4,000 **Unofficial site:** www.thehuddersfield.net
Disabled places: 48

Stadium diagram:
- Lawrence Batley Stand
- St Andrews Road / Travel World Stand
- Panasonic North Stand
- John Smiths Kilner Bank
- St James' Street
- Tickets £14
- Away Supporters

Last 5 Seasons:	Last 5 Managers:
1997: Div 1 - 20th	Neil Warnock (93-95)
1998: Div 1 - 16th	Brian Horton (95-97)
1999: Div 1 - 10th	Peter Jackson (97-99)
2000: Div 1 - 8th	Steve Bruce (99-00)
2001: Div 1 - 22nd	Lou Macari (00-Pre)

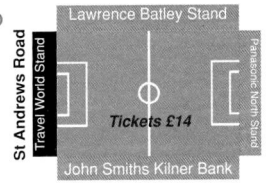

Huddersfield Football Club

Travel:

Rail: Huddersfield 08457 484950

Bus: National Coach Enquiries 0870 6082608

Car: North/East/West:

Exit the M60 at j25, then take the A644 or A62 following signs for Huddersfield. Approximately one mile from the town centre you'll come across the stadium on your left. Turn into Bradley Mills Road and then right after 1/4 mile into Kilner Road, or take the next left into St Andrews Way and left after 1/4 mile into Stadium Way.

South: Come off the M1 at j38 and onto the A637/A642 towards Huddersfield; once you reach the ring road pick up signs for the A62 (Leeds). Once on the A62, turn right into St Andrews Road and then left into Stadium Road. Alternatively take the next right into Bradley Mills Road and then the first right into Kilner Road.

Honours:

Football League: Division 1. Champions: 1923-1924, 1924-1925, 1925-1926. Runners-up: 1926-1927, 1927-1928, 1933-1934.
Division 2. Champions: 1969-1970. Runners-up: 1919-1920, 1952-1953. Promoted from Division 2: 1994-1995 (play-offs).
Division 4. Champions: 1979-1980.

FA Cup: Winners: 1922. Runners-up: 1920, 1928, 1930, 1938.
Football League Cup: Semi-final: 1968.

MY RATING

Date Visited: _____

Rating out of 10:

1 2 3 4 5 6 7 8 9 10

Note: _____

Hull Football Club

Address:
Boothferry Park
Boothferry Road
Hull, HU4 6EU
Switch Board: 01482 575263
Ticket Office: 01482 506666
Website: www.hullcityafc.net
Nickname: The Tigers
Year Formed: 1904

Stands: Hull Daily Mail West Stand, Jones Electrical South Stand, Global Network Solutions East Stand, Boothberry Road North Terrace. Tickets £11-£16

■ *Away Supporters*

Record Attendance: 55,019 v Manchester U Feb, 1949
Record Receipts: £79,604 v Liverpool Feb, 1989
Record League Victory: 11-1 v Carlisle U Jan, 1939
Record Cup Victory: 8-2 v Stalybridge C Nov, 1932
Record Defeat: 0-8 v Wolverhampton W Nov, 1911
Most Capped Player: Terry Neill, 15 Northern Ireland
Most League Appearances: Andy Davidson, 520
Record Transfer Fee Received:
£750,000 for Andy Payton, Nov 1991
Record Transfer Fee Paid:
£200,000 for Peter Swan, Mar 1989
Capacity: 14,819 **Fanzine:** City Ind, err, Amber Necter
Away Capacity: 1,900 **Unofficial site:** www.ambernectar.com
Disabled places: 15

Last 5 Seasons:	Last 5 Managers:
1997: Div 3 - 17th	Stan Ternent (89-91)
1998: Div 3 - 22nd	Terry Dolan (91-97)
1999: Div 3 - 21st	Mark Hateley (97-98)
2000: Div 3 - 14th	Warren Joyce (98-00)
2001: Div 3 - 6th	Brian Little (00-Pre)

Hull City Football Club

Travel:

Rail: Hull Paragon 08457 484950

Bus: National Coach Enquiries 0870 6082608

Car: North: A1 to A1079 (Hull turn-off). Pick up signs for the City Centre until A63. Head towards Leeds on the A63 until you reach Anlaby Road. After about a mile on Anlaby Road you will reach a roundabout, take the first exit for Boothferry Road which leads to the ground.

South: Take the M62 and which becomes the A63 (signposted to Hull) for about 10 miles and then join the A1105. The stadium is approximately 3 miles down the road on the right hand side.

West: M60, then as for South.

Honours:

Football League: Division 2. Best season: 3rd, 1909-1910. Division 3 (N). Champions: 1932-1933, 1948-1949. Division 3. Champions: 1965-1966. Runners-up: 1958-1959. Division 4. Runners-up: 1982-1983.

FA Cup: Semi-final: 1930.

Football League Cup: Best season: 4th, 1974, 1976, 1978.

Associate Members' Cup: Runners-up: 1984.

MY RATING

Date Visited: _____

Rating out of 10:

1 2 3 4 5 6 7 8 9 10

Note: _____

Ipswich Football Club

Address:
Portman Road
Ipswich
Suffolk IP1 2DA

Switch Board: 01473 400500
Ticket Office: 01473 400555
Website: www.itfc.co.uk
Nickname: Town
Year Formed: 1938
Record Attendance: 38,010 v Leeds U Mar, 1975
Record Receipts: £105,950 v AZ May, 1981
Record League Victory: 7-0 v Portsmouth Nov, 1964
Record Cup Victory: 10-0 v Floriana Sep,1962
Record Defeat: 1-10 v Fulham Dec, 1963
Most Capped Player: Allan Hunter, Northern Ireland 47
Most League Appearances: Mick Mills, 591
Record Transfer Fee Received:
£6,000,000 for Kieron Dyer, Jul 1999
Record Transfer Fee Paid:
£4,500,000 for Hermann Hreidarsson, Aug 2000
Capacity: 23,290   **Fanzine:** Those Were the Days
Away Capacity: 3,000 **Unofficial site:** www.twtd.co.uk
Disabled places: 52

Last 5 Seasons:	Last 5 Managers:
1997: Div 1 - 4th	Bobby Robson (69-82)
1998: Div 1 - 5th	Bobby Ferguson (82-87)
1999: Div 1 - 3rd	Johnny Duncan (87-90)
2000: Div 1 - 3rd	John Lyall (90-94)
2001: Prem - 5th	George Burley (94-Pre)

Ipswich Town Football Club

Travel:

Rail: Ipswich 08457 484950

Bus: National Coach Enquiries 0870 6082608

Car: North/West: A14 and take the A1214 (London Road) towards Ipswich West. Follow this road for approx 2 fi miles and at the 2nd set of traffic lights turn right onto A1370 (West End Road). Take a left into Princes Street and then first left onto Portman Road and the ground is on your right.

South: A12, then as above.

MY RATING

Date Visited: _____

Rating out of 10:

1 2 3 4 5 6 7 8 9 10

Note: _____

Honours:

Football League: Division 1. Champions: 1961-1962. Runners-up: 1980-1981, 1981-1982. Promoted from Division 1: 1999-2000 (play-offs). Division 2. Champions. 1960-1961, 1967-1968, 1991-1992. Division 3 (S). Champions: 1953-1954, 1956-1957.

FA Cup: Winners: 1978.

Football League Cup: Semi-final: 1982, 1985.

Texaco Cup: Winners: 1973.

European Competitions:

European Cup: 1962-1963.

European Cup-Winners' Cup: 1978-1979.

UEFA Cup: 1973-1974, 1974-1975, 1975-1976, 1977-1978, 1979-1980, 1980-1981 (winners), 1981-1982, 1982-1983.

Kidderminster Harriers Football Club

Address:
Aggborough Stadium
Hoo Road
Kidderminster
DY10 1NB

Switch Board: 01562 823931
Ticket Office: 01562 823931
Website: www.harriers.co.uk
Nickname: 'Harriers'
Year Formed: 1886
Record Attendance: 9,155 v Hereford Nov, 1948
Record Receipts: Not Disclosed v West Ham United Feb, 1994
Record League Victory: 3-0 v Plymouth Arg Apr, 2001
Record Cup Victory: 10-0 v Brierley Hill Alliance Nov, 1906
Record Defeat: 0-13 v Darwen, 1891
Most Capped Player: Nil
Record Transfer Fee Received:
£380,000 for Lee Hughes, 1997
Record Transfer Fee Paid:
£100,000 for Andy Ducros, July 2000
Capacity: 6,293   **Fanzine:** Mr Harryurz
Away Capacity: 2,000 **Unofficial site:** www.harriers-online.co.uk
Disabled places: Varies

Tickets £7-£13

Away Supporters

Last 5 Seasons:	Last 5 Managers:
1997: Conf - 2nd	Alan Grundy (76-78)
1998: Conf - 17th	John Chambers (78-83)
1999: Conf - 15th	Graham Allner (83-98)
2000: Conf - 1st	P Muller/J Conway (98-99)
2001: Div 3 - 16th	Jan Molby (99-Pre)

Kidderminster Harriers Football Club

Travel:

Rail: Kidderminster
08457 484950

Bus: National Coach
Enquiries 0870 6082608

Car:

From Birmingham, Wolverhampton and North (M5):

Exit the M5 at junction 3(signposted A456) and follow the A456 towards Kidderminster (approximately 12 miles). At roundabout on Kidderminster Ring Road, take first exit (signposted A451 Stourport). At next roundabout, take first exit (signposted A448 Bromsgrove), then take first turning on right (Hoo Road). Aggborough Stadium is approximately half a mile along on the left hand side.

From Worcester and South (M5):

Exit M5 at junction 6 (signposted A449) and follow towards Kidderminster (approximately 15 miles). At first roundabout, take third exit (signposted A449, Kidderminster & Wolverhampton), then take first turning on left before railway bridge. Go down Hoo Road, over railway bridge, and Aggborough Stadium is on the right hand side.

From South-East (M40 & M42)

Leave M5 at junction 4 (signposted A491 Stourbridge). After approximately 5 miles, turn left onto A456 and follow towards Kidderminster. Travel than as from M5.

MY RATING

Date Visited: _____

Rating out of 10:

1 2 3 4 5 6 7 8 9 10

Note: _____
_____
_____
_____

Kidderminster Harriers Football Club

Honours:

Conference: Champions 1993-1994, 1999-2000. Runners-up: 1996-1997.

FA Trophy: 1986-1987 (winners), 1990-1991, 1994-1995 (runners-up).

League Cup: 1996-1997 (winners).

Welsh FA Cup: 1985-1986 (runners-up), 1988-1989 (runners-up).

Conference Fair Play Trophy: (5).

Leeds United Football Club

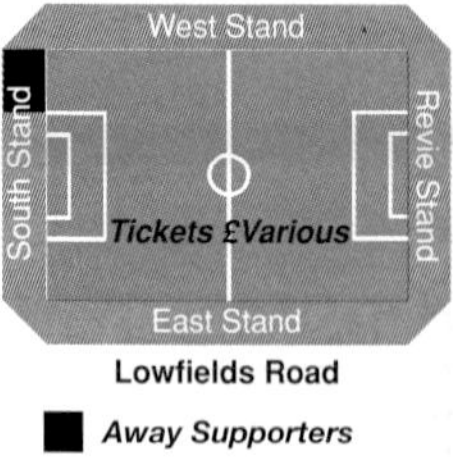

Address:
Elland Road
Leeds
LS11 0ES

Switch Board: 0113 2266000

Ticket Office: 0113 2261000

Website: www.lufc.co.uk

Nickname: The Whites

Year Formed: 1904

Record Attendance: 57,892 v Sunderland Mar, 1967

Record Receipts: £781,445 v Liverpool Jan, 2001

Record League Victory: 8-0 v Leicester C Apr, 1934

Record Cup Victory: 10-0 v Lyn Sep, 1969

Record Defeat: 1-8 v Stoke C Aug, 1934

Most Capped Player: Billy Bremner, Scotland 54

Most League Appearances: Jack Charlton, 629

Record Transfer Fee Received:
£12,000,000 for Jimmy Floyd Hasselbaink, Jul 1999

Record Transfer Fee Paid:
£18,000,000 for Rio Ferdinand, Nov 2000

Capacity: 40,204   **Fanzine:** The Square Ball

Away Capacity: 5,000 **Unofficial site:** www.squareball.co.uk

Disabled places: 280

Last 5 Seasons:	Last 5 Managers:
1997: Prem - 11th	Eddie Gray MBE (82-85)
1998: Prem - 5th	Billy Bremner (85-88)
1999: Prem - 4th	Howard Wilkinson (88-96)
2000: Prem - 3rd	George Graham (96-98)
2001: Prem - 4th	David O'Leary (98-Pre)

Leeds United Football Club

Travel:

Rail: Leeds City 08457 484950

Bus: National Coach Enquiries 0870 6082608

Car:

North: A1, turn off onto the A58 at Wetherby towards Leeds for 13 miles. Turn left onto the A643. Across the M621, turn right into Elland Road. The ground is on the right.

South: M1, continue on the M621 to junction 2, turning left onto the A643, this is Elland Road, then as per North.

West/East: M621, onto the A643 at junction 2. Then as per North.

Honours:

Football League: Division 1. Champions: 1968-1969, 1973-1974, 1991-1992. Runners-up: 1964-1965, 1965-1966, 1969-1970, 1970-1971, 1971-1972. Division 2. Champions: 1923-1924, 1963-1964, 1989-1990. Runners-up: 1927-1928, 1931-1932, 1955-1956.

FA Cup: Winners: 1972. Runners-up: 1965, 1970, 1973.

Football League Cup: Winners: 1968. Runners-up: 1996.

European Competitions:

European Cup: 1969-1970, 1974-1975 (runners-up), 1992-1993, 2000-2001.

European Cup-Winners' Cup: 1972-1973 (runners-up).

European Fairs Cup: 1965-1966, 1966-1967 (runners-up), 1967-1968 (winners), 1968-1969, 1970-1971 (winners).

UEFA Cup: 1971-1972, 1973-1974, 1979-1980, 1995-1996, 1998-1999, 1999-2000 (semi-finalists).

MY RATING

Date Visited: _____

Rating out of 10:

1 2 3 4 5 6 7 8 9 10

Note: _____
_____
_____
_____

Leicester Football Club

Address:

City Stadium
Filbert Street
Leicester, LE2 7FL
Switch Board: 0116 291 5000
Ticket Office: 0116 291 5296
Website: www.lcfc.co.uk
Nickname: The Foxes
Year Formed: 1884
Record Attendance: 47,298 v Tottenham H Feb, 1928
Record Receipts: £377,467 v Aston Villa Feb, 2000
Record League Victory: 10-0 v Portsmouth Oct, 1928
Record Cup Victory: 8-1 v Coventry Dec, 1964
Record Defeat: 0-12 v Nottingham F Apr, 1909
Most Capped Player: John O'Neill, Northern Ireland 39
Most League Appearances: Adam Black, 528
Record Transfer Fee Received:
£11,000,000 for Emile Heskey, Mar 2000
Record Transfer Fee Paid:
£5,000,000 for Ade Akinbiyi, Jul 2000
Capacity: 22,868   **Fanzine:** The Fox
Away Capacity: 2,000 **Unofficial site:** www.forfoxsake.com
Disabled places: 285

Tickets £17

Last 5 Seasons:	Last 5 Managers:
1997: Prem - 9th	Gordon Lee (91)
1998: Prem - 10th	Brian Little (91-94)
1999: Prem - 10th	Mark McGhee (94-95)
2000: Prem - 8th	Martin O'Neill (95-00)
2001: Prem - 13th	Peter Taylor (00-Pre)

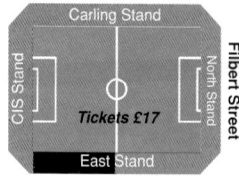

Leicester Football Club

Travel:

Rail: Leicester 0845 7484950

Coach: National Coach Enquiries 0870 6082608

Car: North:

M1 exit at j22 onto A50 towards Leicester. Stay on this as it becomes the A594 and then turns back into the A50 as it becomes part of the ring road. Approximately 9 miles after leaving the motorway turn right into Aylestone Road. Take the first turning on the left into Walnut Street and Filbert Street is just ahead on your right.

South

M1 exit at junction 21 and head for Leicester on the A5460. After 500 Meters you will meet a roundabout, take the second exit staying on the A5460. Travel for 3 Miles, turn right into Upperton Road, cross the river and take the first right for Filbert Street

East

A47, join the ring road, turn right onto the A594 until you join the A50, then as per North.

West:

M69 to junction 21 with M1, get on A5460. Then travel as if going South.

MY RATING

Date Visited: _____

Rating out of 10:

1 2 3 4 5 6 7 8 9 10

Note: _____

Leicester Football Club

Honours:

Football League: Division 1. Runners-up: 1928-1929. Promoted from Division 1. 1993-1994 (play-offs) and 1995-1996 (play-offs). Division 2. Champions. 1924-1925, 1936-1937, 1953-1954, 1956-1957, 1970-1971, 1979-1980. Runners-up: 1907-1908.

FA Cup: Runners-up: 1949, 1961, 1963, 1969.

Football League Cup: Winners: 1964, 1997, 2000. Runners-up: 1965, 1999.

European Competitions:

European Cup-Winners' Cup: 1961-1962.

UEFA Cup: 1997-1998, 2000-2001.

Leyton Orient Football Club

Address:
Matchroom Stadium
Brisbane Road
Leyton
London, E10 5NE
Switch Board: 020 8926 1111
Ticket Office: 020 8926 1111
Website: www.leytonorient.com
Nickname: The O's
Year Formed: 1881
Record Attendance:
34,345 v West Ham U Jan, 1964
Record Receipts: £87,867.92 v West Ham U Jan, 1987
Record League Victory: 8-0 v Crystal Palace Nov, 1955. v Rochdale Oct, 1987. v Colchester U Oct, 1988. v Doncaster R Dec, 1997.
Record Cup Victory: 9-2 v Chester Oct, 1962
Record Defeat: 0-8 v Aston Villa Jan, 1929
Most Capped Player: T Banjo, J Chiedozie Nigeria 7. T Grealish Eire 7.
Most League Appearances: Peter Allen 432
Record Transfer Fee Received:
£600,000 for John Chiedozie, Aug 1981
Record Transfer Fee Paid:
£175,000 for Paul Beesley, Oct 1989
Capacity: 13,842 **Fanzine:** CheeryO's
Away Capacity: 1,400 **Unofficial site:** www.leytonorient-mad.co.uk
Disabled places: 18

Last 5 Seasons:	Last 5 Managers:
1997: Div 3 - 16th	Frank Clark (82-91)
1998: Div 3 - 11th	Peter Eustace (91-94)
1999: Div 3 - 6th	C Turner/J Sitton (94-95)
2000: Div 3 - 19th	Pat Holland (95-96)
2001: Div 3 - 5th	Tommy Taylor (96-Pre)

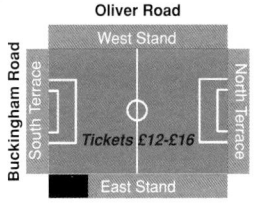

Leyton Orient Football Club

Travel:

Rail: Midland Road
08457 484950

Tube: Leyton (Central Line)

Bus: National Coach Enquiries 0870 6082608

Car:

North: From the M25 come off at junction 27 onto the M11. Follow the M11 South towards London, this runs into the A406 (North Circular), follow Westwards. Take the first exit onto the A104 towards Whipps Cross. At the first roundabout, take the second turning, (signposted Leyton and Stratford). At the junction with Leyton Green Road, turn left and at the end of the road turn left onto Leyton High Road. The ground is approximately 1 mile on the right.

East: A12 into London, Then as per North.

South: A23 to A205 (South Circular), turn right onto A205 (singposted Tulse Hill). Follow signs for Woolwich, turn left onto A207 (Shooters Hill Road). After 1 mile turn right onto the A102(M) through the Blackwall Tunnel. On exiting, take the right hand turning for the A11 (signposted Leytonstone). A quarter of a mile after Maryland station turn left into Chobham Road, and then turn right into the Leyton High Road. A mile later turn left into Ingham Road the ground is on your right.

West: M4, M40/A40 to M25, then as per North.

MY RATING

Date Visited: _____

Rating out of 10:

1 2 3 4 5 6 7 8 9 10

Note: _____

Leyton Orient Football Club

Feature:

Football League: Division 1. Best season: 22nd, 1962-1963. Division 2. Runners-up: 1961-1962. Division 3. Champions: 1969-1970. Division 3 (S). Champions: 1955-1956. Runners-up: 1954-1955. Promoted from Division 4: 1988-1989 (play-offs).

FA Cup: Semi-final: 1978.

Football League Cup: Best season: 5th rd, 1963.

Lincoln City Football Club

Address:
Sincil Bank Stadium
Lincoln
LN5 8LD

Switch Board: 01522 880011
Ticket Office: 01522 880011
Website: www.redimps.com
Nickname: The Red Imps
Year Formed: 1884

Sincil Bank

Simon's Stand
Mundy Stand
Stacey West Stand
Tickets £12
St Andrews Stand

■ *Away Supporters*

Record Attendance: 23,196 v Derby Nov, 1967
Record Receipts: £44,184.46 v Everton Sep, 1993
Record League Victory: 11-1 v Crewe Sep, 1951
Record Cup Victory: 8-1 v Bromley Dec, 1938
Record Defeat: 3-11 v Manchester C Mar, 1895
Most Capped Player: D Pugh, Wales 3, G Moulson, Republic of Ireland 3
Most League Appearances: Tony Emery, 402
Record Transfer Fee Received:
£500,000 for Gareth Ainsworth, Sep 1997
Record Transfer Fee Paid:
£75,000 for Tony Battersby, Aug 1998. For Dean Walling, Sep 1997
Capacity: 10,147   **Fanzine:** Deranged Ferret
Away Capacity: 1,934 **Unofficial site:** www.impsonline.co.uk
Disabled places: 100

Last 5 Seasons:	Last 5 Managers:
1997: Div 3 - 9th	John Beck (95-98)
1998: Div 3 - 3rd	Shane Westley (98)
1999: Div 2 - 23rd	John Reames (98-99)
2000: Div 3 - 15th	Phil Stant (00-01)
2001: Div 3 - 18th	Alan Buckley (01-Pre)

Lincoln City Football Club

Travel:

Rail: Lincoln Central - 0845 7484950

Bus: National Coach Enquiries 0870 6082608

Car:

North: At roundabout which forms the junction with the A46, take 3rd exit. Stay on A46 for 5 miles, over two roundabouts. At 3rd roundabout turn left (signposted Lincoln City FC) into Doddington Road. Straight on for 2 miles to T-junction. Turn left (no signpost) onto Newark Road A1434. Keep on A1434 following Lincoln and City Centre signs. Go straight on (1st exit) at roundabout into the High Street. After 0.5 miles go straight on at lights. After 0.1 miles turn right into Scorer Street.

East: At roundabout which forms junction with A15, take 1st exit onto the A15. Follow Sleaford A1 signs for three miles. On the bridge turn right (signposted Sleaford A15, Grantham A607) onto South Park Avenue. At roundabout after 3 miles turn right (signposted City Centre, Worksop A57) into the High Street. Then as South.

South: Exit the A1 onto the A46. At the roundabout after 9.4 miles take 3rd exit (signposted Lincoln South A1434). Keep on A1434, following 'Lincoln and City Centre' signs for 4.3 miles. Then go straight on (1st exit) at roundabout into the High Street. Continue through a further set of lights and after 0.1 miles turn right into Scorer Street.

MY RATING

Date Visited: _____

Rating out of 10:

1 2 3 4 5 6 7 8 9 10

Note: _____

Lincoln City Football Club

Honours:

Football League: Division 2. Best season: 5th, 1901-1902. Promotion from Division 3. 1997-1998. Division 3 (N). Champions. 1931-1932, 1947-1948, 1951-1952. Runners-up: 1927-1928, 1930-1931, 1936-1937. Division 4. Champions: 1975-1976. Runners-up: 1980-1981.

FA Cup: Best season: 1st rd of Second Series (5th rd equivalent) 1887, 2nd rd (6th rd equivalent), 1890, 1902.

Football League Cup: Best season: 4th rd, 1968.

GM Vauxhall Conference: Champions: 1987-1988.

Liverpool Football Club

Address:
Anfield
Anfield Road
Liverpool, L4 0TH
Switch Board: 0870 2202345
Ticket Office: 0870 2202345
Website: www.liverpoolfc.tv
Nickname: The Reds
Year Formed: 1892
Record Attendance: 61,905 v Wolverhampton W Feb, 1952
Record Receipts: £604,048 v Celtic Sep, 1997
Record League Victory: 10-1 v Rotherham T Feb, 1896
Record Cup Victory: 11-0 v Stromsgodset Sept, 1974
Record Defeat: 1-9 v Birmingham C Dec, 1954
Most Capped Player: Ian Rush 67, Wales
Most League Appearances: Ian Callaghan, 640
Record Transfer Fee Received:
£7,000,000 for Stan Collymore, May 1997
Record Transfer Fee Paid:
£11,000,000 for Emile Heskey, Mar 2000
Capacity: 45,362   **Fanzine:** Through the Wind and The Rain
Away Capacity: Varies   **Unofficial site:** www.koptalk.com
Disabled places: 80

Last 5 Seasons:	Last 5 Managers:
1997: Prem - 4th	Joe Fagan (83-85)
1998: Prem - 3rd	Kenny Dalglish (85-91)
1999: Prem - 7th	Graeme Souness (91-94)
2000: Prem - 4th	Roy Evans (94-98)
2001: Prem - 3rd	Gerard Houllier (98-Pre)

Liverpool Football Club

Travel:

Rail: Kirkdale 08457 484950

Bus: National Coach Enquiries 0870 6082608

Car:

North: Leave the M6 at junction 23 and take the A580 (East Lancashire Rd) to Liverpool. Follow the A580, passing under the M57 (11 miles) then under a railway bridge (2.75 miles) finally, 0.75 mile later turn left onto the A5058 (Queens Drive) towards Widnes. Proceed for 0.5 mile turning right at the lights into Utting Avenue. Pass under the railway bridge into Arkles Lane. The ground is just to the right at the far end of Arkles Lane.

South/East: At the Liverpool end of the M62 follow signs for A5058 (Queens Drive). Stay on the A5058 passing St. Matthews Church (2.5 miles) finally turning left (in 0.5 mile) at the lights into Utting Avenue (Asda is on the right). Pass under the railway bridge which continues into Arkles Lane. The ground is just to the right at the far end of Arkles Lane.

Wales / Wirral: From the end of the M53 or A41, pass through one of the Mersey Tunnels. Whichever tunnel you use you should take the A59 (North/Preston). Follow this road until you see signs for the A580 (St. Helens and Manchester). As you reach the junction where the A59 meets the A580, keep in the right hand lane (A580), which turns right after the lights onto a hill (Everton Valley). Stay in the right hand lane. After the first set of traffic lights turn right onto the A5089 signposted Anfield. Anfield is on the left.

MY RATING

Date Visited: _____

Rating out of 10:

1 2 3 4 5 6 7 8 9 10

Note: _____

Liverpool Football Club

Honours:

Football League: Division 1. Champions: 1900-1901, 1905-1906, 1921-1922, 1922-1923, 1946-1947, 1963-1964, 1965-1966, 1972-1973, 1975-1976, 1976-1977, 1978-1979, 1979-1980, 1981-1982, 1982-1983, 1983-1984, 1985-1986, 1987-1988, 1989-1990. **Runners-up:** 1898-1899, 1909-1910, 1968-1969, 1973-1974, 1974-1975, 1977-1978, 1984-1985, 1986-1987, 1988-1989, 1990-1991. **Division 2. Champions:** 1893-1894, 1895-1896, 1904-1905, 1961-1962.

FA Cup: Winners: 1965, 1974, 1986, 1989, 1992, 2001. **Runners-up:** 1914, 1950, 1971, 1977, 1988, 1996.

Football League Cup: Winners: 1981, 1982, 1983, 1984, 1995, 2001. **Runners-up:** 1978, 1987.

League Super Cup: Winners: 1986.

European Competitions:

European Cup: 1964-1965, 1966-1967, 1973-1974, 1976-1977 (winners), 1977-1978 (winners), 1978-1979, 1979-1980, 1980-1981 (winners), 1981-1982, 1982-1983, 1983-1984 (winners), 1984-1985 (runners-up).

European Cup-Winners' Cup: 1965-1966 (runners-up), 1971-1972, 1974-1975, 1992-1993, 1996-1997 (s-f).

European Fairs Cup: 1967-1968, 1968-1969, 1969-1970, 1970-1971.

UEFA Cup: 1972-1973 (winners), 1975-1976 (winners), 1991-1992, 1995-1996, 1997-1998, 1998-1999, 2000-2001 (winners).

Super Cup: 1977 (winners), 1978, 1984.

World Club Championship: 1981 (runners-up), 1984 (runners up)

Luton Town Football Club

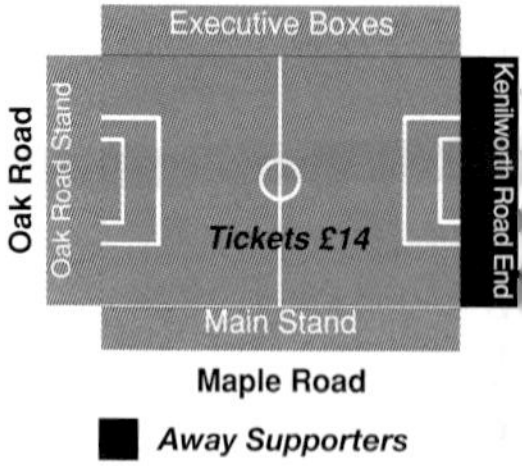

Address:
Kenilworth Road Stadium
1 Maple Road
Luton, LU4 8AW
Switch Board: 01582 411622
Ticket Office: 01582 416976
Website: www.lutontown.co.uk
Nickname: The Hatters
Year Formed: 1885
Record Attendance: 30,069 v Blackpool Mar, 1959
Record Receipts: £115,541.20 v West Ham U Mar, 1994
Record League Victory: 12-0 v Bristol R Apr, 1936
Record Cup Victory: 9-0 v Clapton Nov, 1927
Record Defeat: 0-9 v Small Heath Nov, 1898
Most Capped Player: Mal Donaghy, Northern Ireland 58
Most League Appearances: Bob Morton, 494
Record Transfer Fee Received:
£2,500,000 for John Hartson, Jan 1995
Record Transfer Fee Paid:
£850,000 for Lars Elstrup, Aug 1989
Capacity: 9,975   **Fanzine:** Mad as a hatter
Away Capacity: 2,200 **Unofficial site:** www.lutonfc.com
Disabled places: 32

Last 5 Seasons:	Last 5 Managers:
1997: Div 2 - 3rd	Terry Westley (95)
1998: Div 2 - 17th	Lennie Lawrence (95-00)
1999: Div 2 - 12th	Ricky Hill (00)
2000: Div 2 - 13th	Lil Fuccillo (00)
2001: Div 2 - 22nd	Joe Kinnear (01-Pre)

Luton Town Football Club

Travel:

Rail: Luton 08457 484950

Bus: National Coach Enquiries 0870 6082608

Car:

North/West: Leave the M1 at junction 11 and take the A505 towards Luton. Stay on this road and on encountering the central one way system follow signs for Dunstable. You will eventually see the ground on your left.

South: Take the M1 to junction 10. Follow the signs for the Town Centre, then turn left onto the Inner Ring Road, and continue straight until this becomes the Dunstable Road. Continue under the railway bridge and after about 0.25 mile turn left into Oak Road for the ground.

East: Take the A505 following signs for Luton, once you meet the inner ring road, continue as if travelling South.

Honours:

Football League: Division 1. Best season: 7th, 1986-1987. Division 2. Champions: 1981-1982. Runners-up: 1954-1955, 1973-1974. Division 3. Runners-up: 1969-1970. Division 4. Champions: 1967-1968. Division 3 (S). Champions: 1936-1937. Runners-up: 1935-1936.

FA Cup: Runners-up: 1959. Football League Cup: Winners: 1988. Runners-up: 1989. Simod Cup: Runners-up: 1988.

MY RATING

Date Visited: _____

Rating out of 10:

1 2 3 4 5 6 7 8 9 10

Note: _____
_____
_____
_____

Macclesfield Town Football Club

Address:
Moss Rose Ground
London Road
Macclesfield, SK11 7SP
Switch Board: 01625 264686
Ticket Office: 01625 264686
Website: www.mtfc.co.uk
Nickname: The Silkmen
Year Formed: 1874
Record Attendance: 9008 v Winsford U Feb, 1948
Record Receipts: Undisclosed v Manchester City Sept, 1998
Record League Victory: 5-2 v Mansfield T Nov, 1999
Record Cup Victory: 9-0 v Hartford Saint Johns Nov, 1884
Record Defeat: 1-13 v Tranmere R May, 1929
Most Capped Player: Nil
Most League Appearances: Darren Tinson, 127
Record Transfer Fee Received:
£40,000 for Mike Lake, 1988
Record Transfer Fee Paid:
£30,000 for Efetobore Sodje, Aug 1997
Capacity: 6,028   **Fanzine:** Silkmens News (in Norwegian)
Away Capacity: 2,300 **Unofficial site:** www.thesilkweb.com
Disabled places: 12

Last 5 Seasons:	Last 5 Managers:
1997: Conf - 1st	Roy Campbell (86)
1998: Div 3 - 2nd	Peter Wragg (86-93)
1999: Div 2 - 24th	Sammy McIlroy (93-00)
2000: Div 3 - 13th	Peter Davenport (00)
2001: Div 3 - 14th	Gil Prescott (01-Pre)

Macclesfield Town Football Club

Travel:

Rail: Macclesfield 08457 484950

Bus: National Coach Enquiries 0870 6082608

Car:

North:

Exit the M6 at junction 9 (Knutsford) and follow the A537 to Macclesfield. Follow the signs to the Town Centre. The ground is signposted from the Town Centre but if in doubt follow the signs towards Leek (A523). The ground is about one mile out of town on the A523.

South:

Exit the M6 at junction 17 (Sandbach) and follow the A534 to Congleton. From here take the A536 to Macclesfield (Macclesfield is signposted from the Motorway). After passing the 'Rising Sun' pub on the left continue for about 1/4 of a mile and turn right at the Texaco garage onto Moss Lane. Follow Moss Lane until you reach the ground.

East/West:

Take the A537 into Macclesfield to the junction with the A523. Turn onto the A523 (signposted Leek) and continue for 1.5 miles until you reach the ground.

MY RATING

Date Visited: _____

Rating out of 10:

1 2 3 4 5 6 7 8 9 10

Note: _____

Macclesfield Town Football Club

Honours:

Football League: Division 3. Runners-up: 1997-1998.

FA Cup Best Season: 3rd Round 1968-1988.

Vauxhall Conference: Champions: 1994-1995, 1996-1997.

FA Trophy: Winners: 1969-1970, 1995-1996. Runners-up: 1988-1989.

Bob Lord Trophy: Winners: 1993-1994. Runners-up: 1995-1996, 1996-1997.

Vauxhall Conference Championship Shield: Winners: 1996, 1997, 1998.

Northern Premier League: Winners: 1968-1969, 1969-1970, 1986-1987. Runners-up: 1984-1985.

Northern Premier League Challenge Cup: Winners: 1986-1987. Runners-up: 1969-1970, 1970-1971, 1982-1983.

Northern Premier League Presidents Cup: Winners: 1986-1987. Runners-up: 1984-1985.

Cheshire Senior Cup: Winners 19 times. Runner-up 11 times.

Manchester City Football Club

Address:
Maine Road
Moss Side
Manchester, M14 7WN
Switch Board: 0161 232 3000
Ticket Office: 0161 226 2224
Website: www.mcfc.co.uk
Nickname: The Citizens
Year Formed: 1894
Record Attendance: 84,569 v Stoke C Mar, 1934
Record Receipts: £512,235 Man U v Oldham Ath Apr, 1994
Record League Victory: 10-1 v Huddersfield T Nov, 1987
Record Cup Victory: 10-1 v Swindon T Jan, 1930
Record Defeat: 1-9 v Everton Sept, 1906
Most Capped Player: Colin Bell, England 48
Most League Appearances: Alan Oakes, 565
Record Transfer Fee Received:
£4,925,000 for Georgi Kinkladze, May 1998
Record Transfer Fee Paid:
£3,000,000 for Lee Bradbury, Jul 1997
Capacity: 34,026   **Fanzine:** King of the Kippax
Away Capacity: 2,000 **Unofficial site:** www.service.uit.no/mancity
Disabled places: 88

Maine Road

Away Supporters

Last 5 Seasons:	Last 5 Managers:
1997: Div 1 - 14th	Alan Ball (95-96)
1998: Div 1 - 22nd	Steve Coppell (96)
1999: Div 2 - 3rd	Frank Clark (96-98)
2000: Div 1 - 2nd	Joe Royle (98-01)
2001: Prem - 18th	Kevin Keegan (01-Pre)

Manchester City Football Club

Travel:

Rail: Manchester Piccadilly 08457 484950

Bus: National Coach Enquiries 0870 6082608

Car:

North/West:

M61 and M63, and exit at junction 9 following the signs to Manchester (A5103); turn right at the crossroads (2 3/4 miles) into Claremont Road, after 0.3 miles turn right into Maine Road.

South:

Exit the M6 at junction 19 following the A556 and exit the M56 at junction 3, then follow the directions as if travelling North.

East:

Exit the M62 at junction 17 and take the A56 to the A57 (following signs to Manchester Airport), then follow Birmingham signs to A5103 and turn left into Claremont Road (1.3 miles), then follow the directions as if travelling North.

MY RATING

Date Visited: _____

Rating out of 10:

1 2 3 4 5 6 7 8 9 10

Note: _____

Manchester City Football Club

Honours:

Football League: Division 1. Champions: 1936-1937, 1967-1968. Runners-up: 1903-1904, 1920-1921, 1976-1977, 1999-2000. Division 2. Champions: 1898-1899, 1902-1903, 1909-1910, 1927-1928, 1946-1947, 1965-1966. Runners-up: 1895-1896, 1950-1951, 1987-1988. Promoted from Division 2 (play-offs) 1998-1999.

FA Cup: Winners: 1904, 1934, 1956, 1969. Runners-up: 1926, 1933, 1955, 1981.

Football League Cup: Winners: 1970, 1976. Runners-up: 1974.

European Competitions:

European Cup: 1968-1969.

European Cup-Winners' Cup: 1969-1970 (winners), 1970-1971.

UEFA Cup: 1972-1973, 1976-1977, 1977-1978, 1978-1979.

Manchester United Football Club

Address:
Old Trafford
Sir Matt Busby Way
Manchester, M16 0RA
Switch Board: 0161 868 8000
Ticket Office: 0161 868 8020
Website: www.manutd.com
Nickname: The Red Devils
Year Formed: 1902
Record Attendance: 76,962 Wolves v Grimsby Town Mar, 1939
Record Receipts: £723,650.22 v Liverpool Jan, 1999
Record League Victory: 9-0 v Ipswich Town Mar, 1995
Record Cup Victory: 10-0 v RSC Anderlecht Sept, 1956.
Record Defeat: 0-7 v Blackburn R Apr, 1926. v Aston Villa Dec, 1930. v Wolves Dec 1931.
Most Capped Player: Bobby Charlton, England 106
Most League Appearances: Bobby Charlton, 606
Record Transfer Fee Received:
£16,000,000 for Jap Stam, Sep 2001
Record Transfer Fee Paid:
£28,100,000 for Juan Sebastian Veron, Jul 2001
Capacity: 68,174   **Fanzine:** United we Stand
Away Capacity: 3,200 **Unofficial site:** www.uwsonline.com
Disabled places: 253

Last 5 Seasons:	Last 5 Managers:
1997: Prem - 1st	Frank O'Farrell (71-72)
1998: Prem - 2nd	Tommy Docherty (72-77)
1999: Prem - 1st	Dave Sexton (77-81)
2000: Prem - 1st	Ron Atkinson (81-86)
2001: Prem - 1st	Alex Ferguson (86-Pre)

Manchester United Football Club

Travel:

Rail: Old Trafford 08457 484950

Bus: National Coach Enquiries 0870 6082608

Car:

North:

Approaching on the M61, at junction 1 continue onto the M602 and keep on this road for 4 miles. At junction 3 turn right onto Trafford Road and after 1 mile turn right again into Trafford Park Road. Sir Matt Busby Way and Old Trafford are on the left.

South:

Take the M6 to junction 19, turning onto the A556 Stockport Road which becomes the Chester Road. After 9 miles, turn left onto the A5063 Trafford Road, left onto the A5081 Trafford Park Road and left again into Sir Matt Busby Way. Old Trafford is on the right.

West:

Approaching on the M62, at junction 12 continue on the M602, keeping to this road for 4 miles. Then as route for North.

East:

Get onto the M63 and at junction 7 turn onto the A556. Then as route for South.

MY RATING

Date Visited: _____

Rating out of 10:

1 2 3 4 5 6 7 8 9 10

Note: _____
_____
_____
_____

Manchester United Football Club

Honours:

FA Premier League: Champions: 1992-1993, 1993-1994, 1995-1996, 1998-1999, 1999-2000, 2000-2001. Runners Up: 1994-1995, 1997-1998.

Football League: Division 1. Champions: 1907-1908, 1910-1911 1951-1952, 1955-1956, 1956-57, 1964-65, 1966-1967. Runners-up: 1946-1947, 1947-1948, 1948-1949, 1950-1951, 1958-1959, 1963-1964, 1967-1968, 1979-1980, 1987-1988, 1991-1992.
Division 2. Champions: 1935-1936, 1974-1975. Runners- up: 1896-1897, 1905-1906, 1924-1925, 1937-1938.

FA Cup: Winners 1909, 1948, 1963, 1977, 1983, 1985, 1990, 1994, 1996, 1999. Runners- up: 1957, 1958, 1976, 1979, 1995.

Football League Cup: Winners: 1992. Runners- up: 1983, 1991, 1994.

European Competitions: European Cup: 1956-1957 (sf) 1957-1958 (sf) 1965-1966 (sf) 1967-1968 (Winners), 1968-1969 (sf), 1993-1994, 1994-1995, 1996-1997 (sf) 1997-1998, 1998-1999 (Winners), 1999-2000, 2000-2001(sf). European Cup Winners Cup: 1963-1964, 1977-1978, 1983-1984, 1990-1991(Winners), 1991-1992.

European Fairs Cup: 1964-1965. UEFA Cup: 1976-1977, 1980-1981, 1982-1983, 1984-1985, 1992-1993, 1995-1996. Super Cup 1991 (Winners), 1999 (Runners- Up).

Intercontinental Cup: 1999 (Winners), 1968 (Runners- up).

Mansfield Town Football Club

Address:
Field Mill, Quarry Lane
Mansfield
Notts, NG18 5DA
Switch Board: 01623 482482
Ticket Office: 01623 482482
Website: www.mansfieldtown.net
Nickname: The Stags
Year Formed: 1897
Record Attendance: 24,467 v Nottingham F Jan, 1953
Record Receipts: £46,915 v Sheffield W Jan, 1991
Record League Victory: 9-2 v Rotherham U Dec, 1932
Record Cup Victory: 8-0 v Scarborough Nov, 1952
Record Defeat: 1-8 v Walsall Jan, 1933
Most Capped Player: John McClelland, Northern Ireland 6
Most League Appearances: Rod Arnold, 440
Record Transfer Fee Received:
655,000 for Colin Calderwood, Jul 1993
Record Transfer Fee Paid:
150,000 for Lee Peacock, Oct 1997
Capacity: 9,990   **Fanzine:** Follow the Yellow Brick Road
Away Capacity: 3,000 **Unofficial site:** www.stagsnet.com
Disabled places: 40

Last 5 Seasons:	Last 5 Managers:
1997: Div 3 - 11th	Ian Greaves (83-89)
1998: Div 3 - 12th	George Foster (89-93)
1999: Div 3 - 8th	Andy King (93-96)
2000: Div 3 - 17th	Steve Parkin (96-99)
2001: Div 3 - 13th	Bill Dearden (99-Pre)

Mansfield Town Football Club

Travel:

Rail: Mansfield 08457 484950

Bus: National Coach Enquiries 0870 6082608

Car:

North:

Leave the M1 at junction 29, take the A617 to Mansfield. After 6 miles turn right into Rosemary Street. Follow the road for 1 mile (it becomes the A60 - Portland Road) and turn right into Quarry Lane. The ground is 250 meters on the right.

South:

Leave the M1 at junction 28, take the A38 (Sutton Road) into Mansfield. Continue along this road until you see The Victoria Hospital. Take the third turning on the right and you will enter Belvedere Road. Continue along this until it becomes Portland Road and then travel as if North.

East:

A617 into Mansfield. Turn left into St Peters Way and continue to the end of the road, then left again into Portland Street. Take the third right into Quarry Lane and the ground is 250 meters on the right.

MY RATING

Date Visited: _____

Rating out of 10:

1 2 3 4 5 6 7 8 9 10

Note: _____

Mansfield Town Football Club

Honours:

Football League: Division 2: Best season: 21st, 1977-1978. Division 3. Champions: 1976-1977. Division 4. Champions: 1974-1975. Division 3 (N). Runners-up: 1950-1951.

FA Cup: Best season: 6th rd, 1969.

Football League Cup: Best season: 5th rd, 1976.

Freight Rover Trophy: Winners: 1987.

Middlesbrough Football Club

Address:
BT Cellnet Riverside Stadium
Middlesbrough
TS3 6RS

Switch Board: 01642 877700
Ticket Office: 01642 877700
Website: www.mfc.co.uk
Nickname: Boro
Year Formed: 1876

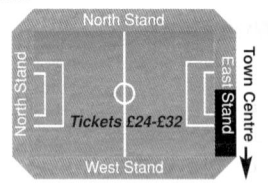

Away Supporters

Record Attendance: Ayresome Park 53,536 v Newcastle U Dec, 1949. BT Cellnet 34,800 v Leeds United Feb, 2000
Record Receipts: £486,229 v Newcastle U Dec, 1998
Record League Victory: 9-0 v Brighton & HA Aug, 1958
Record Cup Victory: 7-0 v Hereford U Sep, 1996
Record Defeat: 0-9 v Blackburn R Nov, 1954
Most Capped Player: Wilf Mannion, England 26
Most League Appearances: Tim Williamson, 563
Record Transfer Fee Received:
£12,000,000 for Juninho, Jul 1997
Record Transfer Fee Paid:
£8,000,000 for Ugo Ehiogu, Oct 2000
Capacity: 35,049   **Fanzine:** Fly me to the Moon
Away Capacity: Varies **Unofficial site:** www.fmttm.com
Disabled places: 360

Last 5 Seasons:	Last 5 Managers:
1997: Prem - 19th	Bruce Rioch (86-90)
1998: Div 1 - 2nd	Colin Todd (90-91)
1999: Prem - 9th	Lennie Lawrence (91-94)
2000: Prem - 12th	Bryan Robson (94-01)
2001: Prem - 14th	Steve McClaren (01-Pre)

Middlesbrough Football Club

Travel:

Rail: Middlesbrough 08457 484950

Bus: National Coach Enquiries 0870 6082608

Car:

North:

Going to Middlesbrough on the A19, cross the River Tees. Turn left onto the A66 bypass. Travel for 3 miles until you reach the first roundabout and then turn right into Forest Road where you will see the ground ahead of you.

South:

Coming from the M1 exit on to the A19 signposted for Teeside. After 30 miles, turn right onto the A66 Middlesbrough bypass. Then travel as North.

West:

A1 (M) to junction 57 which will take you onto the A66 M. This road becomes the A66 and having followed it for 20 Miles you will reach a roundabout where you turn right into Forest Road. The ground is ahead of you.

MY RATING

Date Visited: _____

Rating out of 10:
1 2 3 4 5 6 7 8 9 10

Note: _____

Middlesbrough Football Club

Honours:

Football League: Division 1. Champions: 1994-1995. Runners-up: 1997-1998. Division 2: Champions: 1926-1927, 1928-1929, 1973-1974. Runners-up: 1901-1902, 1991-1992. Division 3: Runners-up: 1966-1967, 1986-1987.

FA Cup: Runners-up: 1997.

Football League Cup: Runners-up: 1997, 1998.

Amateur Cup: Winners: 1895, 1898.

Anglo-Scottish Cup: Winners: 1976.

Zenith Data Systems Cup: Runners-up: 1990.

Millwall Football Club

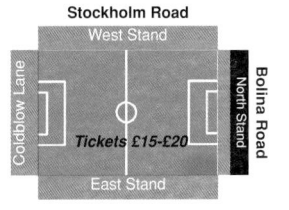

Address:
The Den
Zampa Road
London, SE16 3LN
Switch Board: 020 7232 1222
Ticket Office: 020 7231 9999
Website: www.millwallfc.co.uk
Nickname: The Lions
Year Formed: 1885

Stockholm Road
West Stand
Coldblow Lane
Bolina Road
North Stand
Tickets £15-£20
East Stand

■ *Away Supporters*

Record Attendance: 20,093 v Arsenal Jan, 1994
Record Receipts: Undisclosed
Record League Victory: 9-1 v Torquay U Aug, 1927
Record Cup Victory: 7-0 v Gateshead Dec, 1936
Record Defeat: 1-9 v Aston Villa Jan, 1946
Most Capped Player: Eamonn Dunphy, Republic of Ireland 22
Most League Appearances: Barry Kitchener, 523
Record Transfer Fee Received:
£2,300,000 for Mark Kennedy, Mar 1995
Record Transfer Fee Paid:
£800,000 for Paul Goddard, Dec 1989
Capacity: 20,146 **Fanzine:** The Lion Roars
Away Capacity: 4,000 **Unofficial site:** www.hof.org.uk
Disabled places: 200

Last 5 Seasons:	Last 5 Managers:
1997: Div 2 - 14th	Jimmy Nicholl (96-97)
1998: Div 2 - 18th	John Docherty (97)
1999: Div 2 - 10th	Billy Bonds (97-98)
2000: Div 2 - 5th	Keith Stevens (98-00)
2001: Div 2 - 1st	Mark McGhee (00-Pre)

Millwall Football Club

Travel:

Rail: Bermondsey 08457 484950

Tube: Surrey Quays (East London Line), and New Cross Gate

Bus: National Coach Enquiries 0870 6082608

Car:

North: Follow the M1 to junction 2 and then follow the A1 through Islington. Pick up signs for Shoreditch, Whitechapel, and finally Ring Road. Continue over Tower Bridge and take the first exit at the roundabout onto the A2. Follow the A2 Old Kent Road and after four miles turn left into Ilderton Road. Continue along Ilderton Road until you pass a church on your right, Zampa road is the next on the right.

South: Follow the A20 into London looking for signs to New Cross. At the New Cross follow the signs for the City into Kender Street. Take the first left, turn right at the traffic lights into Ilderton Road, then travel as if going North.

West: Having come off the M4 at junction 2 pick up the A205 at Kew Bridge and follow it towards the East end. You will travel through Putney, Richmond, briefly pick up the A3 at Wandsworth before rejoining the A205 at Clapham Common North Side. Continue following it until it becomes the A202 at Camberwell. Go through Peckham, past Queens Road station and then turn right up Kender Street. Now travel as if going South.

MY RATING

Date Visited: _____

Rating out of 10:
1 2 3 4 5 6 7 8 9 10

Note: _____

Millwall Football Club

Honours:

Football League: Division 1. Best season: 3rd, 1993-1994.
Division 2. Champions: 1987-1988, 2001-2001 Division 3 (S).
Champions 1927-1928, 1937-1938. Runners-up: 1952-1953.
Division 3. Runners-up: 1965-1966, 1984-1985. Division 4.
Champions: 1961-1962. Runners-up: 1964-1965.

FA Cup: Semi-final: 1900, 1903, 1937.

Football League Cup: Best season: 5th rd, 1974, 1977, 1995.

Football League Trophy: Winners: 1983.

Auto Windscreens Shield: Runners-up: 1999

Newcastle United Football Club

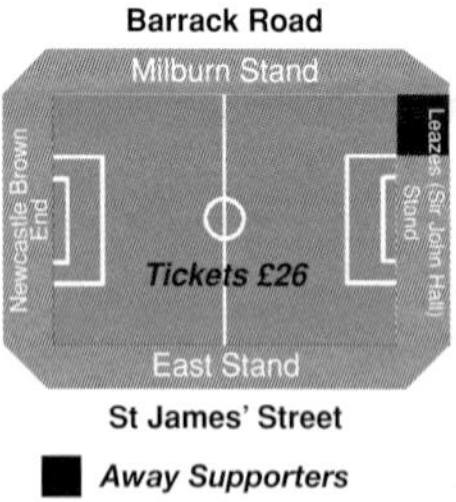

Address:
St James' Park
Newcastle upon Tyne
NE1 4ST

Switch Board: 0191 201 8400

Ticket Office: 0191 261 1571

Website: www.nufc.co.uk

Nickname: The Magpies

Year Formed: 1882

Record Attendance: 68,386 v Chelsea Sep, 1930

Record Receipts: £830,271 v Everton Mar, 1999

Record League Victory: 13-0 v Newport Oct, 1946

Record Cup Victory: 9-0 v Southport Feb, 1932

Record Defeat: 0-9 v Burton Wanderers Apr, 1895

Most Capped Player: Alf McMichael, Northern Ireland 40

Most League Appearances: Jim Lawrence, 432

Record Transfer Fee Received:
£8,000,000 for Dieter Hamann, Jul 1999

Record Transfer Fee Paid:
£15,000,000 for Alan Shearer, Jul 1996

Capacity: 52,218   Fanzine: The Mag, True Faith

Away Capacity: Varies Unofficial site: www.nufc.com

Disabled places: 103

Last 5 Seasons:	Last 5 Managers:
1997: Prem - 2nd	Ossie Ardiles (91-92)
1998: Prem - 13th	Kevin Keegan (92-97)
1999: Prem - 13th	Kenny Dalglish (97-98)
2000: Prem - 11th	Ruud Gullit (98-99)
2001: Prem - 11th	Bobby Robson (99-Pre)

Newcastle United Football Club

Travel:

Rail: Central Station
08457 484950

Bus: National Coach
Enquiries 0870 6082608

Car:

North:

Exit the A1 onto the A167 Ponteland Road heading for the city centre. After 1.5 miles at the fourth roundabout turn left onto Jedburgh Road. Take the first right turn onto Grandstand Road and then left onto the A189 Ponteland Road. Continue along this road which becomes Barrack road. The ground is on the left.

South:

From the A1(M), keep on the A1 as the road divides. Turn onto the A184 at the junction and continue along the road bearing left onto the A189 after 1.5 miles. Continue over the Tyne over the Redheugh Bridge which then becomes St James' Boulevard. After 0.5 Miles turn left at Gallowgate roundabout and the stadium is on the right.

MY RATING

Date Visited: _____

Rating out of 10:

1 2 3 4 5 6 7 8 9 10

Note: _____
_____
_____
_____

Newcastle United Football Club

Honours:

FA Premier League: Runners-up: 1995-1996, 1996-1997.

Football League: Division 1. Champions: 1904-1905, 1906-1907, 1908-1909, 1926-1927, 1992-1993. **Division 2. Champions:** 1964-1965. **Runners-up:** 1897-1898, 1947-1948.

FA Cup: Winners: 1910, 1924, 1932, 1951, 1952, 1955. **Runners-up:** 1905, 1906, 1908, 1911, 1974, 1998, 1999.

Football League Cup: Runners-up: 1976.

Texaco Cup: Winners: 1974, 1975.

European Competitions:

European Cup: 1997-1998.

European Fairs Cup: 1968-1969 (winners), 1969-1970, 1970-1971.

UEFA Cup: 1977-1978, 1994-1995, 1996-1997.

European Cup Winners' Cup: 1998-1999.

Anglo-Italian Cup: Winners: 1972-1973.

Northampton Town Football Club

Address:
Sixfields Stadium
Upton Way
Northampton, NN5 5QA
Switch Board: 01604 757773
Ticket Office: 01604 588338
Website: www.ntfc.co.uk
Nickname: The Cobblers
Year Formed: 1897

■ *Away Supporters*

Record Attendance: County Ground 24,523 v Fulham Apr, 1966.
Sixfields 7,557 Manchester City Sept, 1998.
Record Receipts: £102,979 v Tottenham H Oct, 1998
Record League Victory: 10-0 v Walsall Nov, 1927
Record Cup Victory: 10-0 v Sutton T Dec, 1907
Record Defeat: 0-11 v Southampton Dec, 1901
Most Capped Player: E Lloyd Davies, Wales 12
Most League Appearances: Tommy Fowler, 521
Record Transfer Fee Received:
£265,000 for Richard Hill, Jul 1987
Record Transfer Fee Paid:
£150,000 for Jamie Forrester, Jul 2000
Capacity: 7,653   **Fanzine:** What a Load of Cobblers
Away Capacity: 1,500 **Unofficial site:** www.ntfcunofficial.com
Disabled places: 77

Last 5 Seasons:	Last 5 Managers:
1997: Div 3 - 4th	Theo Foley (90-92)
1998: Div 2 - 4th	Phil Chard (92-93)
1999: Div 2 - 22nd	John Barnwell (93-95)
2000: Div 3 - 3rd	Ian Atkins (95-99)
2001: Div 2 - 18th	Kevin Wilson (99-Pre)

Northampton Town Football Club

Travel:

Rail: Northampton Station 08457 484950

Bus: National Coach Enquiries 0870 6082608

Car:

East: Take A45 into Northampton. Turn off at roundabout signposted Hardingstone and take 4th exit, heading for Mereway. Go straight on at the next two roundabouts. At the 3rd roundabout take 3rd exit, heading away from Oxford. At the next roundabout turn right into the Sixfields leisure complex and the ground is directly in front of you.

North: When you reach the Ring road, travel clockwise and then follow directions as if you were coming from the East.

West: Take the A45 into Northampton and follow the ring road around and then follow directions as if you were coming from the East.

Honours:

Football League: Division 1. Best season: 21st, 1965-1966. Division 2. Runners-up: 1964-1965. Division 3. Champions: 1962-1963. Promoted from Division 3. 1996-1997 (play-offs). Division 3 (S). Runners-up: 1927-1928, 1949-1950. Division 4. Champions: 1986-1987. Runners-up: 1975-1976.

FA Cup: Best season: 5th rd, 1934, 1950, 1970.

Football League Cup: Best season: 5th rd, 1965, 1967.

MY RATING

Date Visited: _____

Rating out of 10:

1 2 3 4 5 6 7 8 9 10

Note: _____

Norwich City Football Club

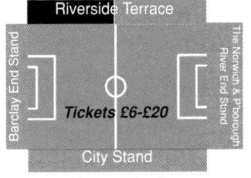

Address:
Carrow Road
Norwich
Norfolk, NR1 1JE
Switch Board: 01603 760760
Ticket Office: 01603 761661
Website: www.canaries.co.uk
Nickname: The Canaries
Year Formed: 1902
Record Attendance: 43,984 v Leicester C Mar, 1963
Record Receipts: £261,918 v Internazionale Nov, 1993
Record League Victory: 10-2 v Coventry C Mar, 1930
Record Cup Victory: 8-0 v Sutton Jan, 1989
Record Defeat: 2-10 v Swindon T Sep, 1908
Most Capped Player: Mark Bowen Wales, 35
Most League Appearances: Ron Ashman, 592
Record Transfer Fee Received:
£5,000,000 for Chris Sutton, Jul 1994
Record Transfer Fee Paid:
£1,000,000 for Jon Newsome, Jun 1994
Capacity: 21,468   **Fanzine:** Scrimmage
Away Capacity: 2,000 **Unofficial site:** www.pinkun.com
Disabled places: 115

Last 5 Seasons:	Last 5 Managers:
1997: Div 1 - 13th	Gary Megson (95-96)
1998: Div 1 - 15th	Mike Walker (96-98)
1999: Div 1 - 9th	Bruce Rioch (98-00)
2000: Div 1 - 12th	Bryan Hamilton (00)
2001: Div 1 - 15th	Nigel Worthington (01-Pre)

Norwich City Football Club

Travel:

Rail: Norwich 08457 484950

Bus: National Coach Enquiries 0870 6082608

Car:

North: Having followed the A140. Turn left onto the A47 outer ring road. Follow the outer ring road until it becomes Harvey Lane. At the bottom of Harvey Lane turn right into Thrope Road and after 400 Meters turn left into Carrow Road. Continue along Carrow Road and you will see the ground.

South: From the A11 or A140, turn right onto the A47 towards Great Yarmouth and Lowestoft. Take the A146 Norwich/Lowestoft sliproad and then turn left towards Norwich. Continue for a further mile and then onto the A1054. After 300 Meters you will see Carrow Road. Turn into the road and continue for 300 Meters and you will see the ground.

Honours:

FA Premier League: Best season: 3rd 1992-1993. Football League: Division 2. Champions: 1971-1972, 1985-1986. Division 3 (S). Champions: 1933-1934. Division 3. Runners-up: 1959-1960.

FA Cup: Semi-finals: 1959, 1989, 1992. Football League Cup: Winners: 1962, 1985. Runners-up: 1973, 1975.

European Competitions: UEFA Cup: 1993-1994.

MY RATING

Date Visited: _____

Rating out of 10:

1 2 3 4 5 6 7 8 9 10

Note: _____

Nottingham Forest Football Club

Address:
The City Ground
Nottingham
NG2 5FJ
Switch Board: 0115 982 4444
Ticket Office: 0115 982 4445
Website: www.nottinghamforest.co.uk
Nickname: The Reds, Forest
Year Formed: 1865

Away Supporters

Record Attendance: 49,946 v Manchester U Oct, 1967
Record Receipts: £499,099 v Bayern Munich Mar, 1996
Record League Victory: 12-0 v Leicester Fosse Apr, 1909
Record Cup Victory: 14-0 v Clapton Jan, 1891
Record Defeat: 1-9 v Blackburn R Apr, 1937
Most Capped Player: Stuart Pearce, England 76
Most League Appearances: Bob McKinlay, 614
Record Transfer Fee Received:
£8,500,000 for Stan Collymore, Jun 1995
Record Transfer Fee Paid:
£3,500,000 for Pierre van Hooijdonk, Mar 1997
Capacity: 30,602   **Fanzine:** Forest Fever
Away Capacity: 3,000 **Unofficial site:** www.trentend.co.uk
Disabled places: 67

Last 5 Seasons:	Last 5 Managers:
1997: Prem - 20th	Stuart Pearce (96-97)
1998: Div 1 - 1st	Dave Bassett (97-98)
1999: Prem - 20th	Ron Atkinson (98-99)
2000: Div 1 - 14th	David Platt (99-01)
2001: Div 1 - 11th	Paul Hart (01-Pre)

Nottingham Forest Football Club

Travel:

Rail: Nottingham Midland 08457 484950

Bus: National Coach Enquiries 0870 6082608

Car:

North: **M1 to junction 26, following the signs to Nottingham via the A610 to the A6514 at Western Boulevard. Turn right and follow the Ring Road South, where the Ring Road becomes the A52. Continue South on the A52 over the Clifton Bridge which joins the Lings Bar Road at the next traffic island. Continue to the Gamston Island and then turn left into Radcliffe Road (A6011). Turn right into Colwick Road.**

South: **M1 to junction 24, on the A453 towards Nottingham. At the Clifton Bridge complex follow signs for the A52 Grantham past Nottingham Knight Island to join the Lings Bar Road at the next traffic island. Follow the A52 signposted Grantham to the Gamston Island and then turn left into Radcliffe Road (A6011). Turn right into Colwick Road.**

East: **Following the A52 Radcliffe Road from Grantham. At Gamston Island continue along Radcliffe Road as it becomes the A6011. Turn right into Colwick Road.**

West: **Approach via the A52 from Derby to the Nottingham Ring Road, turn right onto the Ring Road (A52) and follow as above.**

MY RATING

Date Visited: _____

Rating out of 10:
1 2 3 4 5 6 7 8 9 10

Note: _____

Nottingham Forest Football Club

Honours:

Football League: Division 1. Champions: 1977-1978, 1997-1998. Runners-up: 1966-1967, 1978-1979. Division 2. Champions: 1906-1907, 1921-1922. Runners-up: 1956-1957. Division 3 (S). Champions: 1950-1951.

FA Cup: Winners: 1898, 1959. Runners-up: 1991.

Football League Cup: Winners: 1978, 1979, 1989, 1990. Runners-up: 1980, 1992.

Anglo-Scottish Cup: Winners: 1977.

Simod Cup: Winners: 1989.

Zenith Data Systems Cup: Winners: 1992.

European Competitions:

European Fairs Cup: 1961-1962, 1967-1968.

European Cup: 1978-1979 (winners), 1979-1980 (winners), 1980-1981.

Super Cup: 1979-1980 (winners), 1980-1981 (runners-up).

World Club Championship: 1980.

UEFA Cup: 1983-1984, 1984-1985, 1995-1996.

Notts County Football Club

Address:
Meadow Lane
Nottingham
NG2 3HJ
Switch Board: 0115 952 9000
Ticket Office: 0115 955 7210
Website: www.nottscountyfc.co.uk
Nickname: The Magpies
Year Formed: 1862
Record Attendance: 47,310 v York Mar, 1955
Record Receipts: £124,539.10 v Manchester C Feb, 1991
Record League Victory: 11-1 v Newport Co Jan, 1949
Record Cup Victory: 15-0 v Rotherham T Oct, 1885
Record Defeat: 1-9 v Blackburn R Nov, 1889. v Aston Villa Sep, 1888. v Portsmouth Apr, 1927
Most Capped Player: Kevin Wilson, Northern Ireland 15
Most League Appearances: Albert Iremonger, 564
Record Transfer Fee Received:
£2,500,000 for Craig Short, Sep 1992
Record Transfer Fee Paid:
£685,000 for Tony Agana, Nov 1991
Capacity: 20,300   **Fanzine:** The Pie, No More Pie In The Sky
Away Capacity: 5,438 **Unofficial site:** www.nottscounty.net
Disabled places: 60

Last 5 Seasons:	Last 5 Managers:
1997: Div 2 - 24th	Colin Murphy (95)
1998: Div 3 - 1st	Steve Thompson (96)
1999: Div 2 - 16th	Sam Allardyce (97-99)
2000: Div 2 - 8th	Gary Brazil (99-00)
2001: Div 2 - 8th	Jocky Scott (00-Pre)

Notts County Football Club

Travel:

Rail: Nottingham Midland
08457 484950

Bus: National Coach
Enquiries 0870 6082608

Car:

North: Leave the M1 at junction 26 and take the A610 towards Nottingham and then follow the signs for Melton Mowbray. Turn left before the River Trent into Meadow Lane. The ground is 200yd on the left.

East: Take the A52 Radcliffe Road into Nottingham, and follow signs for Trent Bridge. As you approach the city centre, at the intersection; bear left (which remains the Radcliffe Road). At the next T-junction; turn right and cross the river. Take the second left to Meadow Lane, continue down Meadow Lane and you will see the ground.

South: Take the M1 to junction 24. Take the A453 and follow signs for Trent Bridge as you approach the city. The A453 crosses the A60 (Loughborough Road) as you enter Nottingham, turn left here still (signposted for Trent Bridge) and follow the A60 across the river and then take the second left into meadow lane.

West: Take the A52 into Nottingham picking up signs for Melton Mowbray and then Trent Bridge (A606). Then travel as if going North.

MY RATING

Date Visited: _____

Rating out of 10:

1 2 3 4 5 6 7 8 9 10

Note: _____
_____
_____
_____

Notts County Football Club

Honours:

Football League: Division 1. Best season: 3rd, 1890-1891, 1900-1901. Division 2. Champions: 1896-1897, 1913-1914, 1922-1923. Runners-up: 1894-1895, 1980-1981. Promoted from Division 2: 1990-1991 (play-offs). Division 3 (S). Champions: 1930-1931, 1949-1950. Runners-up: 1936-1937. Division 3. Champions: 1997-1998. Runners-up: 1972-1973. Promoted from Division 3: 1989-1990 (play-offs). Division 4. Champions: 1970-1971. Runners-up: 1959-1960.

FA Cup: Winners: 1894. Runners-up: 1891.

Football League Cup: Best season: 5th rd, 1964, 1973, 1976.

Anglo-Italian Cup: Winners: 1995. Runners-up: 1994.

Oldham Athletic Football Club

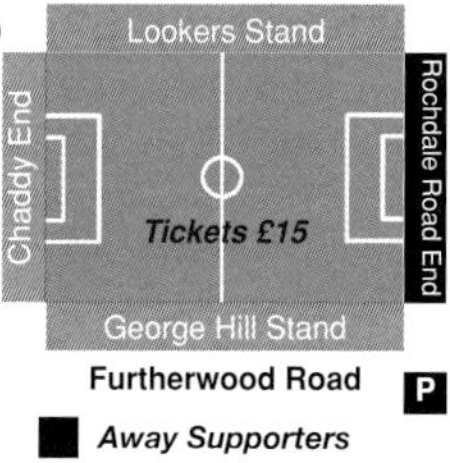

Address:
Boundary Park
Oldham
OL1 2PA
Switch Board: 0161 627 4972
Ticket Office: 0161 624 4972
Website: www.oldhamathletic.co.uk
Nickname: The Latics
Year Formed: 1895
Record Attendance: 47,671 v Sheffield W Jan, 1930
Record Receipts: £138,680 v Manchester U Dec, 1993
Record League Victory: 11-0 v Southport Dec, 1962
Record Cup Victory: 10-1 v Lytham Nov, 1925
Record Defeat: 4-13 v Tranmere R Dec, 1935
Most Capped Player: Gunnar Halle, Norway 24
Most League Appearances: Ian Wood, 525
Record Transfer Fee Received:
£1,700,000 for Earl Barrett, Feb 1992
Record Transfer Fee Paid:
£750,000 for Ian Olney, Jun 1992
Capacity: 13,559   **Fanzine:** Beyond the Boundary
Away Capacity: 4,600 **Unofficial site:** www.oafc.co.uk
Disabled places: 52

Last 5 Seasons:	Last 5 Managers:
1997: Div 1 - 23rd	Jimmy Frizzell (70-82)
1998: Div 2 - 13th	Joe Royle (82-94)
1999: Div 2 - 20th	Graeme Sharp (94-97)
2000: Div 2 - 14th	Neil Warnock (97-98)
2001: Div 2 - 15th	Andy Ritchie (98-Pre)

Oldham Athletic Football Club

Travel:

Rail: Oldham Werneth 08457 484950

Bus: National Coach Enquiries 0870 6082608

Car:

From all Directions:

Leave M62 at junction 20 and take the A627 (M) towards Oldham. Leave A627 (M) at 2nd exit and at the big roundabout take the second exit signposted Oldham and Ashton. After approximately half a mile at the traffic lights turn left and continue along the road past the new B&Q warehouse on your right. At the mini roundabout turn left into Furtherwood Road. Continue down the road and you will see the ground ahead of you.

Honours:

Football League: Division 1. Runners-up: 1914-1915. Division 2 Champions: 1990-1991. Runners-up: 1909-1910. Division 3 (N). Champions: 1952-1953. Division 3. Champions: 1973-1974. Division 4. Runners-up: 1962-1963.

FA Cup: Semi-final: 1913, 1990, 1994.

Football League Cup: Runners-up: 1990.

MY RATING

Date Visited: _____

Rating out of 10:
1 2 3 4 5 6 7 8 9 10

Note: _____

Oxford United Football Club

Address:
The Kassam Stadium
Oxford
OX4 4XR
Switch Board: 01865 337500
Ticket Office: 01865 337533
Website: www.oufc.co.uk
Nickname: The U's
Year Formed: 1893
Record Attendance: 22,730 v Preston NE Feb, 1964
Record Receipts: £136,423 v Chelsea Jan, 1999
Record League Victory: 7-0 v Barrow Dec, 1964
Record Cup Victory: 9-1 v Dorchester T Nov, 1995
Record Defeat: 0-7 v Sunderland Sep, 1998
Most Capped Player: Jim Magilton, Northern Ireland 18
Most League Appearances: John Shuker, 478
Record Transfer Fee Received:
£1,600,000 for Matt Elliott, Jan 1997
Record Transfer Fee Paid:
£475,000 for Dean Windass, Aug 1998
Capacity: 12,500 **Fanzine:** Rage On
Away Capacity: 5,000 **Unofficial site:** www.rageonline.co.uk
Disabled places: Varies

Last 5 Seasons:	Last 5 Managers:
1997: Div 1 - 17th	Malcolm Crosby (97)
1998: Div 1 - 12th	Malcolm Shotton (98-99)
1999: Div 1 - 23rd	Denis Smith (00)
2000: Div 2 - 20th	David Kemp (00-01)
2001: Div 2 - 24th	Mark Wright (01-Pre)

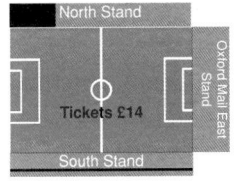

Oxford United Football Club

Rail: Oxford 08457 484950

Bus: National Coach Enquiries 0870 6082608

Car, North: **Exit the M40 at junction 9. Follow the A34 until you reach a roundabout. Turn left at the roundabout and follow the ring road (A40) clockwise. At the** Headington roundabout continue straight on (now the A4142). After 2 miles you will see the Rover car factory on your left. Exit the ring road and go down the slip road to the roundabout. Turn left at that roundabout and continue as though you are going out of town as this road takes you directly to the Kassam Stadium.

East: Leave the M40 at junction 8 to join the A40, signposted Oxford. Continue on the A40, go straight on at the lights until you come to the Green Road roundabout. Take the first exit, signposted Ring Road (A4142). After two sets of traffic lights you will see the Rover car factory on your left. Then as North.

South: From the A34 join the Oxford Ring Road at the South Hinksey interchange. Turn right on the ring road following signs for Cowley(A4142). At a large roundabout you will see Sainsburys on the far side. Take the road for Sandford on Thames at that roundabout and continue for half a mile until you see a turn for the Science Park. Turn into the Science Park and go across a couple of roundabouts. The Kassam Stadium is on your left.

MY RATING

Date Visited: _____

Rating out of 10:

1 2 3 4 5 6 7 8 9 10

Note: _____

Oxford United Football Club

Honours:

Football League: Division 1. Best season: 12th, 1997-1998. Division 2. Champions: 1984-1985. Runners-up: 1995-1996. Division 3. Champions: 1967-1968, 1983-1984. Division 4. Promoted 1964-1965 (4th).

FA Cup: Best season: 6th rd, 1964.

Football League Cup: Winners: 1986.

Peterborough United Football Club

Address:
London Road Ground
Peterborough
Cambridgeshire, PE2 8AL
Switch Board: 01733 563947
Ticket Office: 01733 563947
Website: www.theposh.com
Nickname: Posh
Year Formed: 1923
Record Attendance: 30,096 v Swansea T Feb, 1965
Record Receipts: £51,315 v Brighton & HA Feb, 1986
Record League Victory: 9-1 v Barnet Sep, 1998
Record Cup Victory: 7-0 v Harlow T Nov, 1991
Record Defeat: 1-8 v Northampton T Dec, 1946
Most Capped Player: Tony Millington, Wales 8
Most League Appearances: Tommy Robson, 482
Record Transfer Fee Received:
£700,000 for Simon Davies, Dec 1999
Record Transfer Fee Paid:
£350,000 for Martin O'Connor, Jul 1996
Capacity: 15,314 **Fanzine:** The Peterborough Effect
Away Capacity: 4,495 **Unofficial site:** www.posh.net
Disabled places: 40

Last 5 Seasons:	Last 5 Managers:
1997: Div 2 - 21st	Chris Turner (91-92)
1998: Div 3 - 10th	Lil Fuccillo (92-93)
1999: Div 3 - 9th	John Still (94-95)
2000: Div 3 - 5th	Mick Halsall (95-96)
2001: Div 2 - 12th	Barry Fry (96-Pre)

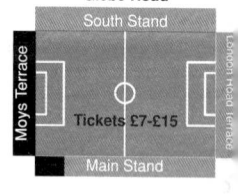

Peterborough United Football Club

Travel:

Rail: Peterborough
08457 484950

Bus: National Coach
Enquiries 0870 6082608

Car:

North:

Following the A1, Exit the A1 at signpost 'Leicester, Peterborough North A47'. Turn left at T-junction onto the A47. Exit the A47 after 5 miles, at junction 15 and at the roundabout turn right onto the A1260 Nene Parkway. Exit the Nene Parkway after 1 mile and at the mini-roundabout by the 'Gordon Arms' turn left onto the A605 Oundle Road. Continue for just under two miles until you get to a roundabout; take the third exit onto London Road, and the ground is on the left.

South:

Take the A1 to the roundabout with the A15. Take the London Road (signposted Peterborough A15) until you get to a large intersection at which you should turn left (continuing along London Road) and the ground is immediately on the right.

East:

Following the A47, pass through the village of Eye following signs to Peterborough A47. At the roundabout turn left and at the next roundabout turn right. At the following roundabout take the 2nd exit. Then as from North.

MY RATING

Date Visited: _____

Rating out of 10:

1 2 3 4 5 6 7 8 9 10

Note: _____
_____
_____
_____

Peterborough United Football Club

Honours:

Football League: Division 1. Best season: 10th. 1992-1993. Promoted from Division 3. 1999-2000 (play-offs).

Division 4. Champions: 1960-1961, 1973-1974.

FA Cup: Best season: 6th rd, 1965.

Football League Cup: Semi-final: 1966.

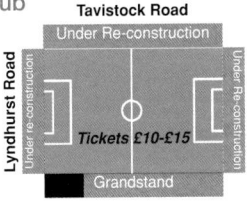

Plymouth Argyle Football Club

Address:
Home Park
Plymouth
Devon, PL2 3DQ

Switch Board: 01752 562561
Ticket Office: 01752 562561
Website: www.pafc.co.uk
Nickname: The Pilgrims
Year Formed: 1886
Record Attendance: 43,596 v Aston Villa Oct, 1936
Record Receipts: £128,000 v Burnley May, 1994
Record league Victory: 8-1 v Millwall Jan, 1932. v Hartlepool United May, 1994
Record Cup Victory: 6-0 v Corby T Jan, 1966
Record Defeat: 0-9 v Stoke C Dec, 1960
Most Capped Player: Moses Russell, Wales 20
Most League Appearances: Kevin Hodges, 530
Record Transfer Fee Received: £750,000 for Mickey Evans, Mar 1997
Record Transfer Fee Paid: £250,000 for Paul Dalton, Jun 1992
Capacity: 19,630 (7,300 during redevelopment)
Fanzine: Rub of the Greens
Away Capacity: 2,760 (100 during redevelopment)
Unofficial site: www.rubofthegreens.com **Disabled places:** 48

Last 5 Seasons:	Last 5 Managers:
1997: Div 2 - 19th	Steve McCall (95)
1998: Div 2 - 22nd	Neil Warnock (95-97)
1999: Div 3 - 13th	Mick Jones (97-98)
2000: Div 3 - 12th	Kevin Hodges (98-00)
2001: Div 3 - 12th	Paul Sturrock (00-Pre)

Plymouth Argyle Football Club

Travel:

Rail: Plymouth North Road 08457 484950

Bus: National Coach Enquiries 0870 6082608

Car:

North/East:

Take the M5 to the South West and at the end of the motorway continue onto the A38. On going into Plymouth, turn left onto the A386 (Tavistock Road) - towards Plymouth. This road will then branch into two, keep on the left hand side (signposted Plymouth) and after about a mile you will see the ground on your left.

West:

Follow the A38 or A388 onto the A386 (Tavistock Road). Then travel as if going North/East.

Honours:

Football League: Division 2. Best season: 4th, 1931-1932, 1952 1953. Division 3 (S). Champions: 1929-1930, 1951-1952. Runners-up: 1921-1922, 1922-1923, 1923-1924, 1924-1925, 1925-1926, 1926-1927. Division 3. Champions: 1958-1959. Runners-up: 1974-1975, 1985-1986. Promoted: 1995-1996 (play offs).

FA Cup: Semi-final: 1984. Football League Cup: Semi-final: 1965, 1974.

MY RATING

Date Visited: _____

Rating out of 10:

1 2 3 4 5 6 7 8 9 10

Note: _____

Port Vale Football Club

Address:
Vale Park
Hamil Road
Burslem
Stoke-on-Trent, ST6 1AW
Switch Board: 01782 835524
Ticket Office: 01782 811707
Website: www.port-vale.co.uk
Nickname: The Valiants
Year Formed: 1876
Record Attendance: 49,768 v Aston Villa Oct, 1936
Record Receipts: £170,349 v Everton Feb, 1996
Record League Victory: 9-1 v Chesterfield Sep, 1932
Record Cup Victory: 7-1 v Irthlingborough Jan, 1907
Record Defeat: 0-10 v Sheffield U Dec, 1892
Most Capped Player: Tony Rougier, Trinidad and Tobago
Most League Appearances: Roy Sproson, 761
Record Transfer Fee Received:
£2,000,000 for Gareth Ainsworth, Oct 1998
Record Transfer Fee Paid:
£500,000 for Gareth Ainsworth, Sep 1997
Capacity: 20,000   **Fanzine:** The Beano
Away Capacity: 4,500 **Unofficial site:** www.onevalefan.co.uk
Disabled places: 200

Last 5 Seasons:	Last 5 Managers:
1997: Div 1 - 8th	Dennis Butler (78-79)
1998: Div 1 - 19th	Alan Bloor (79)
1999: Div 1 - 21st	John McGrath (80-83)
2000: Div 1 - 23rd	John Rudge (84-99)
2001: Div 2 - 11th	Brian Horton (99-Pre)

Port Vale Football Club

Travel:

Rail: Longport 08457 484950

Bus: National Coach Enquiries 0870 6082608

Car:

MY RATING

Date Visited: _____

Rating out of 10:
1 2 3 4 5 6 7 8 9 10

Note: _____

North: Leave M6 at junction 16 and take the A500 South to Stoke on Trent. After 6 miles take the Tunstall exit (A527). At the roundabout take the second exit (signposted Tunstall A527). After half a mile turn right at the small roundabout on to the B501 (second exit, Newcastle Street). Go straight on at the next roundabout and across the next cross roads into Moorland Road. Take the second left on to Hamil Road and Vale park is on the left.

South: Leave the M6 at junction 15 and take the A500 North to Stoke on Trent. Continue straight across the two large roundabouts on the A500 heading North. After the second roundabout take the fourth exit sign posted Tunstall (A527). At the roundabout turn right (fourth exit sign posted A527 Tunstall, Longport Road). After 0.5 miles turn right on to the B501 and then continue as North.

West: Follow the A500 East and take the exit sign posted Tunstall A527. At the roundabout take the left turning (second exit sign posted A527 Tunstall, Longport Road). After 0.5 miles turn right on to the B501 and then continue as North.

Port Vale Football Club

Honours:

Football League: Division 2. Runners-up: 1993-1994. Division 3 (N). Champions: 1929-1930, 1953-1954. Runners-up: 1952-1953. Division 4. Champions: 1958-1959. Promoted 1969-1970 (4th).

FA Cup: Semi-final: 1954.

Football League Cup: Best season: 3rd rd 1992, 1997.

Autoglass Trophy: Winners: 1993.

Anglo-Italian Cup: Runners-up: 1996.

LDV Vans Trophy: Winners 2001.

Portsmouth Football Club

Address:
Fratton Park
Frogmore Road
Portsmouth
Hampshire, PO4 8RA
Switch Board: 02392 731204
Ticket Office: 02392 618777
Website: www.pompeyfc.co.uk
Nickname: Pompey
Year Formed: 1898
Record Attendance: 51,385 v Derby Co Feb, 1949
Record Receipts: £233,000 v Chelsea Mar, 1997
Record League Victory: 9-1 v Notts Co Apr, 1927
Record Cup Victory: 7-0 v Stockport Co Jan, 1949
Record Defeat: 0-10 v Leicester C Oct, 1928
Most Capped Player: Jimmy Dickinson, England 48
Most League Appearances: Jimmy Dickinson, 764
Record Transfer Fee Received:
£3,500,000 for Lee Bradbury, Aug 1997
Record Transfer Fee Paid:
£1,000,000 for Rory Allen, Jul 1999
Capacity: 19,179 **Fanzine:** Pisces
Away Capacity: 3,000 **Unofficial site:** www.portsmouth-mad.co.uk
Disabled places: 35

Last 5 Seasons:	Last 5 Managers:
1997: Div 1 - 7th	Terry Fenwick (95-98)
1998: Div 1 - 20th	Alan Ball (98-99)
1999: Div 1 - 19th	Tony Pulis (00)
2000: Div 1 - 18th	Steve Claridge (00-01)
2001: Div 1 - 20th	Graham Rix (01-Pre)

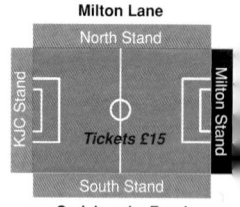

Portsmouth Football Club

Travel:

Rail: Fratton 08457 484950

Bus: National Coach Enquiries 0870 6082608

Car:

From all Directions:

From either the A3 (M) or M27 travel until you reach the A2030 signposted for Southsea. Turn right or left on to the A2030 (which is dual carriageway nearly all the way) then continue until you reach a roundabout at the end of Velder Avenue. The ground is directly ahead of you.

Honours:

Football League: Division 1. Champions: 1948-1949, 1949-1950. Division 2. Runners-up: 1926-1927, 1986-1987. Division 3 (S). Champions: 1923-1924. Division 3. Champions: 1961-1962, 1982-1983.

FA Cup: Winners: 1939. Runners-up: 1929, 1934.

Football League Cup: Best season: 5th rd, 1961, 1986.

MY RATING

Date Visited: _____

Rating out of 10:
1 2 3 4 5 6 7 8 9 10

Note: _____

Preston North End Football Club

Address:
Deepdale
Sir Tom Finney Way
Preston, PR1 6RU
Switch Board: 01772 902020
Ticket Office: 01772 902222
Website: www.pnefc.net
Nickname: The Lilywhites
Year Formed: 1881
Record Attendance: 42,684 v Arsenal Apr, 1938
Record Receipts: £108,920 v Stockport C Jan, 2001
Record League Victory: 10-0 v Stoke Sep, 1889
Record Cup Victory: 26-0 v Hyde Oct, 1887
Record Defeat: 0-7 v Blackpool May, 1948
Most Capped Player: Tom Finney, England 76
Most League Appearances: Alan Kelly, 447
Record Transfer Fee Received:
£1,250,000 for Kevin Kilbane, Jun 1997
Record Transfer Fee Paid:
£1,500,000 for David Healy, Dec 00
Capacity: Redeveloping - will be 25,000 on completion
Fanzine: Raising The Coffin
Away Capacity: Varies **Unofficial site:** www.pnefans.com
Disabled places: Varies

Last 5 Seasons:	Last 5 Managers:
1997: Div 2 - 15th	John McGrath (86-90)
1998: Div 2 - 15th	Les Chapman (90-92)
1999: Div 2 - 5th	John Beck (92-94)
2000: Div 2 - 1st	Gary Peters (94-98)
2001: Div 1 - 4th	David Moyes (98-Pre)

Preston North End Football Club

Travel:

Rail: Preston 08457 484950

Bus: National Coach Enquiries 0870 6082608

Car:

From All directions:

Exit the M6 at junction 31. At the roundabout take the first exit (signposted Preston A59) onto the A59. After 1 mile at the mini roundabout by the Hesketh Arms, take the second exit (signposted ring road, Blackpool A583, Football Ground) onto the Blackpool Road A5085. Carry straight on for 1.2 miles, then filter left before the lights (signposted Town Centre, Football Ground) into Sir Tom Finney Way. The ground is on the left-hand-side.

MY RATING

Date Visited: _____

Rating out of 10:

1 2 3 4 5 6 7 8 9 10

Note: _____

Honours:

Football League: Division 1. Champions: 1888-1889, 1889-1890. Runners-up: 1890-1891, 1891-1892, 1892-1893, 1905-1906, 1952-1953, 1957-1958. Division 2. Champions: 1903-1904, 1912-1913, 1950-1951, 1999-2000. Runners-up: 1914-1915, 1933-1934. Division 3. Champions: 1970-1971, 1995-1996. Division 4. Runners-up: 1986-1987.

FA Cup: Winners: 1889, 1938. Runners-up: 1888, 1922, 1937, 1954, 1964.

Double Performed: 1888-1889. Football League Cup: Best season: 4th rd, 1963, 1966, 1972, 1981.

Queens Park Rangers Football Club

Address:
Loftus Road Stadium
South Africa Road
London, W12 7PA
Switch Board: 020 8743 0262
Ticket Office: 020 8740 0262
Website: www.qpr.co.uk
Nickname: The R's
Year Formed: 1885

Record Attendance: 35,353 v Leeds U Apr, 1974
Record Receipts: £218,475 v Manchester U Feb, 1994
Record League Victory: 9-2 v Tranmere Dec, 1960
Record Cup Victory: 8-1 v Bristol R Nov, 1937
Record Defeat: 1-8 v Mansfield T Mar, 1965. v Manchester U Mar,1969
Most Capped Player: Alan McDonald, Northern Ireland 52
Most League Appearances: Tiny Ingham, 519
Record Transfer Fee Received:
£6,000,000 for Les Ferdinand, Jun 1995
Record Transfer Fee Paid:
£2,750,000 for Mike Sheron, Jul 1997
Capacity: 19,148   **Fanzine:** A Kick up The R's
Away Capacity: 3,873 **Unofficial site:** www.alternativeqpr.com
Disabled places: 20

Last 5 Seasons:	Last 5 Managers:
1997: Div 1 - 9th	Ray Wilkins (94-96)
1998: Div 1 - 21st	Stewart Houston (96-97)
1999: Div 1 - 20th	Ray Harford (97-98)
2000: Div 1 - 10th	Gerry Francis (98-01)
2001: Div 1 - 23rd	Ian Holloway (01-Pre)

Queens Park Rangers Football Club

Travel:

Rail: Paddington 08457 484950

Tube: White City (Central Line)

Bus: National Coach Enquiries 0870 6082608

Car:

North:

From the M1 take the A406 West, then A40 at Hanger Lane to Central London. Turn off to White City, turn right into Wood Lane, then turn right into the South Africa Road where you will see the ground ahead of you.

East:

A40(M) Westway, then turn off to White City, left into Wood Lane, then turn right into South Africa Road.

South:

Go to the A3 and follow signs for Hammersmith, then take the A219 to Shepherds Bush, then towards White City (Wood Lane), and left into South Africa Road.

West:

Take the M4 to Chiswick, A315 and A402 to Shepherds Bush, then towards White City (Wood Lane), and left into South Africa Road.

MY RATING

Date Visited: _____

Rating out of 10:

1 2 3 4 5 6 7 8 9 10

Note: _____

Queens Park Rangers Football Club

Honours:

Football League: Division 1. Runners-up: 1975-1976. Division 2. Champions: 1982-1983. Runners-up: 1967-1968, 1972-1973. Division 3 (S). Champions: 1947-1948. Runners-up: 1946-1947. Division 3. Champions: 1966-1967.

FA Cup: Runners-up: 1982.

Football League Cup: Winners: 1967. Runners-up: 1986

European Competitions:

UEFA Cup: 1976-1977, 1984-1985.

Reading Football Club

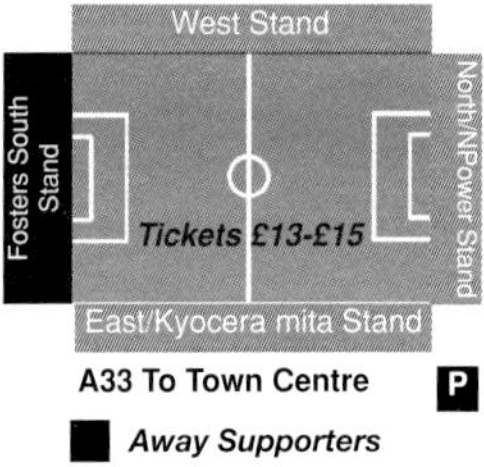

Address:
Madejski Stadium
Bennet Road
Reading
Berks, RG2 0FL
Switch Board: 0118 968 1100
Ticket Office: 0118 968 1000
Website: www.readingfc.co.uk
Nickname: The Royals
Year Formed: 1871
Record Attendance: 33,042 v Brentford Feb, 1927
Record Receipts: £171,203 v Manchester C Mar, 1999
Record League Victory: 10-2 v Crystal Palace Sep, 1946
Record Cup Victory: 6-0 v Leyton Dec, 1925
Record Defeat: 0-18 v Preston NE, 1893
Most Capped Player: Jimmy Quinn, Northern Ireland 17
Most League Appearances: Martin Hicks, 500
Record Transfer Fee Received:
£1,575,000 for Shaka Hislop, Aug 1995
Record Transfer Fee Paid:
£800,000 for Carl Asaba, Aug 1997. Martin Butler, Feb 2000
Capacity: 24,200 **Fanzine:** The Whiff
Away Capacity: 4,000 **Unofficial site:** www.royals.org
Disabled places: 128

Tickets £13-£15
A33 To Town Centre
Away Supporters

Last 5 Seasons:	Last 5 Managers:
1997: Div 1 - 18th	Mark McGhee (91-94)
1998: Div 1 - 24th	J Quinn/M Gooding (94-97)
1999: Div 2 - 11th	Terry Bullivant (97-98)
2000: Div 2 - 10th	Tommy Burns (98-99)
2001: Div 2 - 3rd	Alan Pardew (99-Pre)

Reading Football Club

Travel:

Rail: Reading General 08457 484950

Bus: National Coach Enquiries 0870 6082608

Car:

East/West:

If you are travelling along the M4 from the West you can see the stadium on your left (from the East - the right!) bear left on to the A33 relief road which leads you directly to the stadium.

North: Take the M25 to junction 15 and then join the M4. Then as East/West.

South: Take the M3 to junction 6 and join the A33. Follow this North and cross the M4 at junction 11. Travel then as East/West.

Honours:

Football League: Division 1. Runners-up: 1994-1995. Division 2. Champions: 1993-1994. Division 3. Champions: 1985-1986. Division 3 (S). Champions: 1925-1926. Runners-up: 1931-1932, 1934-1935, 1948-1949, 1951-1952. Division 4. Champions: 1978-1979.

FA Cup: Semi-final: 1927.

Football League Cup: Best season: 5th rd, 1996.

Simod Cup: Winners: 1988.

MY RATING

Date Visited: _____

Rating out of 10:

1 2 3 4 5 6 7 8 9 10

Note: _____

Rochdale Football Club

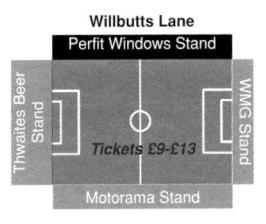

Address:
Spotland Stadium
Sandy Lane
Rochdale, OL11 5DS
Switch Board: 01706 644648
Ticket Office: 01706 644648
Website: www.rochdaleafc.co.uk
Nickname: The Dale
Year Formed: 1900
Record Attendance: 24,231 v Notts County Dec, 1949
Record Receipts: £46,000 v Burnley May, 1992
Record League Victory: 8-1 v Chesterfield Dec, 1926
Record Cup Victory: 8-2 v Crook T Nov, 1927
Record Defeat: 1-9 v Tranmere R Dec, 1931
Most Capped Player: Nil
Most League Appearances: Graham Smith, 317
Record Transfer Fee Received:
£400,000 for Stephen Bywater, Aug 1998
Record Transfer Fee Paid:
£100,000 for Clive Platt, Sep 1999
Capacity: 10,249   **Fanzine:** None Available
Away Capacity: 3,800 **Unofficial site:** www.rochdaleafc.com
Disabled places: 28

Last 5 Seasons:	Last 5 Managers:
1997: Div 3 - 14th	Terry Dolan (89-91)
1998: Div 3 - 18th	Dave Sutton (91-94)
1999: Div 3 - 19th	Mick Docherty (95-96)
2000: Div 3 - 10th	Graham Barrow (96-99)
2001: Div 3 - 8th	Steve Parkin (99-Pre)

Rochdale Football Club

Travel:

Rail: Rochdale 08457 484950

Bus: National Coach Enquiries 0870 6082608

Car:

From all Directions:

Spotland Stadium is best approached from all directions by using the M62. Exiting at junction 20 you should follow signs for Rochdale A627(M). Bear left at the first roundabout and you will come on to the A627(M), passing B&Q on your right. You will quickly approach another roundabout at which point you will pick up signs for 'Spotland Stadium'. However, should you miss these signs you should carry straight on at the roundabout, and after around 2 miles on this road you will come across the ground on your right-hand side.

Honours:

Football League: Division 3. Best season: 9th, 1969-1970. Division 3 (N). Runners-up: 1923-1924, 1926-1927.

FA Cup: Best season: 5th rd, 1990.

Football League Cup: Runners-up: 1962.

MY RATING

Date Visited: _____

Rating out of 10:

1 2 3 4 5 6 7 8 9 10

Note: _____

Rotherham United Football Club

Address:
Millmoor Ground
Rotherham
S60 1HR
Switch Board: 01709 512434
Ticket Office: 01709 309440
Website: www.themillers.co.uk
Nickname: The Merry Millers
Year Formed: 1870
Record Attendance: 25,170 v Sheffield U Dec, 1952. v Sheffield W Jan, 1952.
Record Receipts: £79,155 v Newcastle U Jan, 1993
Record League Victory: 8-0 v Oldham Ath May, 1947
Record Cup Victory: 6-0 v Spennymoor U Dec, 1977. v Wolves Nov, 1985. v Kings Lynn Dec, 1997
Record Defeat: 1-11 v Bradford C Aug, 1928
Most Capped Player: Shaun Goater, Bermuda 19
Most League Appearances: Danny Williams, 459
Record Transfer Fee Received:
£325,000 for Matt Clarke, Jul 1996
Record Transfer Fee Paid:
£150,000 for Tony Towner, Aug 1980. Lee Glover, Aug 1996.
Capacity: 11,514   **Fanzine:** Moulin Rouge
Away Capacity: 2,155 **Unofficial site:** www.supermillers.co.uk
Disabled places: 18

Last 5 Seasons:	Last 5 Managers:
1997: Div 2 - 23rd	Billy McEwan (88-91)
1998: Div 3 - 9th	Phil Henson (91-94)
1999: Div 3 - 5th	Gemmill / McGovern (94-96)
2000: Div 3 - 2nd	Danny Bergara (96-97)
2001: Div 2 - 2nd	Ronnie Moore (97-Pre)

Rotherham United Football Club

Travel:

Rail: Rotherham Central 08457 484950

Bus: National Coach Enquiries 0870 6082608

Car:

North & West: Exit M1 at junction 34. At the roundabout take the second exit, sign-posted Rotherham (A6109). Follow Meadow Bank Road for approx 1.5 miles, turn right at the traffic lights onto Kimberworth Road. At the T-junction after approx 0.5 miles turn left over Centenary bridge to ground.

South: Exit M1 at junction 33. At roundabout turn right onto the Rotherway, sign-posted Rotherham A630. At roundabout turn left onto West Bawtry Road. Follow for approx 0.5 miles until next roundabout, turn right. Follow road approx 1.5 miles, go straight on at Ickles roundabout, (sign-posted Doncaster A630, Barnsley). At Masborough roundabout after approx 0.5 miles turn left to ground.

South & East: Exit the M18 at junction 1, signposted Rotherham A631. Follow signs to Sheffield (A631) for approx 4.5 miles, over the Wickersley, Brecks and Worrygoose Roundabouts to the Rotherway roundabout. Here go straight on following the A630 West Bawtry Road to Rotherham. Then travel as South.

MY RATING

Date Visited: _____

Rating out of 10:

1 2 3 4 5 6 7 8 9 10

Note: _____

Rotherham United Football Club

Honours:

Football League: Division 2. Runners-up 2000-2001, Best season: 3rd, 1954-1955 (equal points with champions and runners-up). Division 3. Champions: 1980-1981. Runners-up: 1999-2000. Division 3 (N). Champions: 1950-1951. Runners-up: 1946-1947, 1947-1948, 1948-1949. Division 4. Champions: 1988-1989. Runners-up: 1991-1992.

FA Cup: Best season: 5th rd, 1953, 1968.

Football League Cup: Runners-up: 1961.

Auto Windscreens Shield: Winners: 1996.

Rushden & Diamonds Football Club

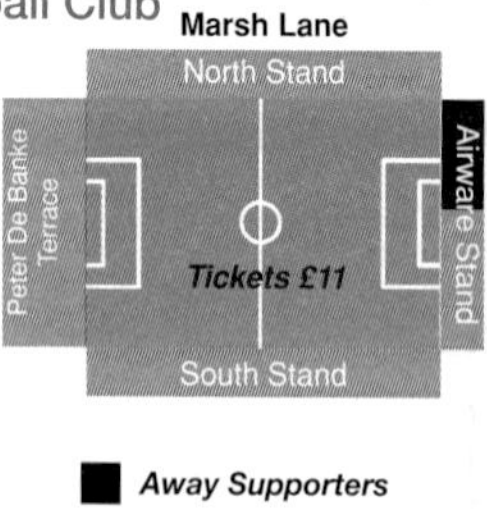

Address:
Nene Park
Diamond Way
Irthlingborough
Northants, NN9 5QF

Switch Board: 01933 652000
Ticket Office: 01933 652936
Website: www.thediamondsfc.com
Nickname: The Diamonds
Year Formed: 1992
Record Attendance: 6,431 v Leeds U Jan, 1999
Record Receipts: £38,276 v Leeds U Jan, 1999
Record League Victory: 7-0 v Redditch May, 1994
Record Cup Victory: 8-0 v Desborough T Sep, 1994
Record Defeat: 0-5 v Slough Town Aug, 1996
Most Capped Player: Nil
Most League Appearances: Garry Butterworth, 254
Record Transfer Fee Received:
£25,000 for Darren Collins, Nov 2000
Record Transfer Fee Paid:
Undisclosed for Justin Jackson, Jul 2000
Capacity: 6,553   Fanzine: Rushin and Rantin
Away Capacity: Varies Unofficial site: www.thediamondsfc.co.uk
Disabled places: 70

Last 5 Seasons:	Last 5 Managers:
1997: Conf - 12th	
1998: Conf - 4th	
1999: Conf - 4th	
2000: Conf - 2nd	Roger Ashby (92-97)
2001: Conf - 1st	Brian Talbot (97-Pre)

Rushden & Diamonds Football Club

Travel:

Rail: Wellingborough Station 08457 484950

Bus: National Coach Enquiries 0870 6082608

Car:

MY RATING

Date Visited: _____

Rating out of 10:

1 2 3 4 5 6 7 8 9 10

Note: _____
_____
_____
_____

North: **Leave the M1/M6 at junction 19 of the M1. Follow the A14 Eastwards, past Neasby and around Kettering until you reach the junction with the A6 (signposted Kettering, Rushden and Bedford.) Follow the A6 towards Rushden and Bedford, around Burton, Latimer and Finedon, and join the Irthlingborough bypass, still signposted towards Rushden and Bedford. At a roundabout on the bypass you will see a sign to the left reading 'Nene Park', the ground is visable from here.**

South: Leave the M1 at junction 15 (signposted Northampton A508) and follow signs to Northampton. After approximately 3 miles, turn right at A45 and follow signs to Wellingborough (A45). Keep on the A45 travelling East, until you reach the junction with the A6, and turn left (signposted Kettering A6). Cross the river and turn right at the next roundabout into the ground.

East: From the A14 follow signs for the M1/M6 and Midlands until you reach the junction with the A45 at Thrapston. Follow the A45 (formerly A605) South Westwards, follow signs for Wellingborough and Northampton until you reach the junction with the A6. Turn right (signposted Kettering A6) over the river and then right at the next roundabout and the ground is in front of you.

Rushden & Diamonds Football Club

Honours:

Conference: Champions: 2000-2001.

Southern League Midland Division: Champions: 1993-1994.

FA Trophy: Semi-finalists 1994.

Northants FA Hillier Senior Cup - Winners: 1993-1994, 1998-1999.

Maunsell Premier Cup - Winners: 1994-1995, 1998-1999.

Scunthorpe United Football Club

Address:
Glanford Park
Doncaster Road
Scunthorpe
North Lincolnshire, DN15 8TD
Switch Board: 01724 848077
Ticket Office: 01724 848077
Website: www.scunthorpe-united.co.uk
Nickname: The Irons
Year Formed: 1899
Record Attendance: 23,935 v Portsmouth Jan,1954 (Old Showground). 8,775 v Rotherham United May, 1989 (Glanford Pk)
Record Receipts: £47,252 v Burnley May, 2000
Record League Victory: 8-1 v Luton Apr, 1965. v Torquay Oct, 1995
Record Cup Victory: 9-0 v Boston U Nov, 1953
Record Defeat: 0-8 v Carlisle U Dec, 1952
Most Capped Player: Nil
Most League Appearances: Jack Brownsword 595
Record Transfer Fee Received:
£350,000 for Neil Cox, Feb 1991
Record Transfer Fee Paid:
£200,000 for Steve Torpey, Feb 2000
Capacity: 9,183   **Fanzine:** Iron-Bru
Away Capacity: 1,643 **Unofficial site:** www.iron-bru.net
Disabled places: 16

Last 5 Seasons:	Last 5 Managers:
1997: Div 3 - 13th	Bill Green (91-93)
1998: Div 3 - 8th	Richard Money (93-94)
1999: Div 3 - 4th	David Moore (94-96)
2000: Div 2 - 23rd	Mick Buxton (96-97)
2001: Div 3 - 10th	Brian Laws (97-Pre)

Scunthorpe United Football Club

Travel:

Rail: Scunthorpe 08457 484950

Bus: National Coach Enquiries 0870 6082608

Car:

From all Directions:

Leave the M180 at junction 3 and take the M181 for Scunthorpe. At the end of this motorway, you will see the ground on your right. Turn right at the first roundabout onto the A18 and right again into the large car park at the ground.

Honours:

Football League: Division 2: Best season: 4th, 1961-1962. Division 3 (N). Champions: 1957-1958. Promoted from Division 3, 1998-1999 (play-offs).

FA Cup: Best season: 5th rd, 1958, 1970.

Football League Cup: Never past 3rd round

MY RATING

Date Visited: _____

Rating out of 10:
1 2 3 4 5 6 7 8 9 10

Note: _____

Sheffield United Football Club

Address:
Bramall Lane
Sheffield
S2 4SU

Switch Board: 0114 2215757
Ticket Office: 0114 2213131
Website: www.sufc.co.uk
Nickname: The Blades
Year Formed: 1889

John Street

Tickets £12-£20

■ *Away Supporters*

Record Attendance: 68,287 v Leeds U Feb, 1936
Record Receipts: £298,364 v Coventry C Mar, 1998
Record League Victory: 10-0 v Burslem Port Vale Dec, 1892
Record Cup Victory: 5-0 v Newcastle U Jan, 1914. v Corinthians Jan, 1925. v Barrow Jan, 1956.
Record Defeat: 0-13 v Bolton W Feb, 1890
Most Capped Player: Billy Gillespie, Northern Ireland 25
Most League Appearances: Joe Shaw, 629
Record Transfer Fee Received:
£2,700,000 for Brian Deane, Jul 1993
Record Transfer Fee Paid:
£1,200,000 for Don Hutchison, Jan 1996
Capacity: 30,936   **Fanzine:** Flashing Blade
Away Capacity: 5,500 **Disabled places:** 55
Unofficial site: www.sheffieldunited-mad.co.uk

Last 5 Seasons:	Last 5 Managers:
1997: Div 1 - 5th	Howard Kendall (95-97)
1998: Div 1 - 6th	Nigel Spackman (97-98)
1999: Div 1 - 8th	Steve Bruce (98-99)
2000: Div 1 - 16th	Adrian Heath (99)
2001: Div 1 - 10th	Neil Warnock (99-Pre)

Sheffield United Football Club

Travel:

Rail: Sheffield Midland
08457 484950

Bus: National Coach
Enquiries 0870 6082608

Car:

North: From the M1 come off at junction 33 and follow the A57 towards Sheffield. When you reach the Park Square roundabout take the exit onto the A61. Follow the A61 which becomes Shoreham Street (you will need to bear right). At the end of Shoreham Street take a right turn into St Mary's Road, go left at the roundabout by the church and you will see the ground.

South: Come off the M1 at junction 29 and follow the A617 (signposted Chesterfield). After 5 miles, go right onto the A61 (signposted Sheffield). Travel for 10 miles and then bear left onto the A621 - you will be able to see the ground on your right.

Honours:

Football League: Division 1. Champions: 1897-1898. Runners-up: 1896-1897, 1899-1900. Division 2: Champions: 1952-1953. Runners-up: 1892-1893, 1938-1939, 1960-1961, 1970-1971, 1989-1990. Division 4. Champions: 1981-1982.

FA Cup: Winners: 1899, 1902, 1915, 1925. Runners-up: 1901, 1936.

Football League Cup: Best season: 5th rd, 1962, 1967, 1972.

MY RATING

Date Visited: _____

Rating out of 10:
1 2 3 4 5 6 7 8 9 10

Note: _____

Sheffield Wednesday Football Club

Address:
Hillsborough
Sheffield
S6 1SW

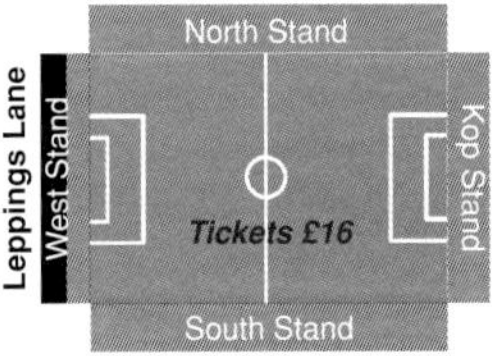

Switch Board: 0114 221 2121
Ticket Office: 0114 221 2400
Website: www.swfc.co.uk
Nickname: The Owls
Year Formed: 1867

■ *Away Supporters*

Record Attendance: 72,841 v Manchester C Feb, 1934
Record Receipts: £533,918 Sunderland v Norwich Apr, 1992
Record League Victory: 9-1 v Birmingham Dec, 1930
Record Cup Victory: 12-0 v Halliwell Jan, 1891
Record Defeat: 0-10 v Aston Villa Oct, 1912
Most Capped Player: Nigel Worthington Northern Ireland, 50
Most League Appearances: Andy Wilson, 502
Record Transfer Fee Received:
£2,650,000 for Paul Warhurst, Sept 1993
Record Transfer Fee Paid:
£4,700,000 for Paolo Di Canio, Aug 1997
Capacity: 39,859   **Fanzine:** Spitting Feathers
Away Capacity: 3,800 **Unofficial site:** www.sheffwed.co.uk
Disabled places: 100

Last 5 Seasons:	Last 5 Managers:
1997: Prem - 7th	Ron Atkinson (97-98)
1998: Prem - 16th	Danny Wilson (98-00)
1999: Prem - 12th	Peter Shreeves (Acting) (00)
2000: Prem - 19th	Paul Jewell (00-01)
2001: Div 1 - 17th	Peter Shreeves (01-Pre)

Sheffield Wednesday Football Club

Travel:

Rail: Sheffield Midland
08457 484950

Bus: National Coach
Enquiries 0870 6082608

Car:

North/South/East:

Exit the M1 at junction 36 and follow the A61 towards Sheffield.
Continue along the road for approximately 4 miles until the second roundabout. Take the third exit (Leppings Lane) and th ground is situated on the left-hand side.

West:

Take the A57 for Sheffield. As you approach the city the road splits in two - take the left fork onto the Rivelin Valley Road (A6101). Continue for approximately 3.75 miles, turn left (onto the one way system) and follow the road round to the right onto Holme Lane. This road then becomes Bradfield Road. At the junction with the A61 Penistone Road, turn left towards Barnsley. Hillsborough Stadium is on the left-hand side after Hillsborough Park.

MY RATING

Date Visited: _____

Rating out of 10:
1 2 3 4 5 6 7 8 9 10

Note: _____

Sheffield Wednesday Football Club

Honours:

Football League: Division 1. Champions: 1902-1903, 1903-1904, 1928-1929, 1929-1930. Runners-up: 1960-1961. Division 2: Champions: 1899-1900, 1925-1926, 1951-1952, 1955-1956, 1958-1959. Runners-up: 1949-1950, 1983-1984.

FA Cup: Winners: 1896, 1907, 1935. Runners-up: 1890, 1966, 1993.

Football League Cup: Winners: 1991. Runners-up: 1993.

European Competitions:

European Fairs Cup: 1961-1962, 1963-1964.

UEFA Cup: 1992-1993.

Shrewsbury Town Football Club

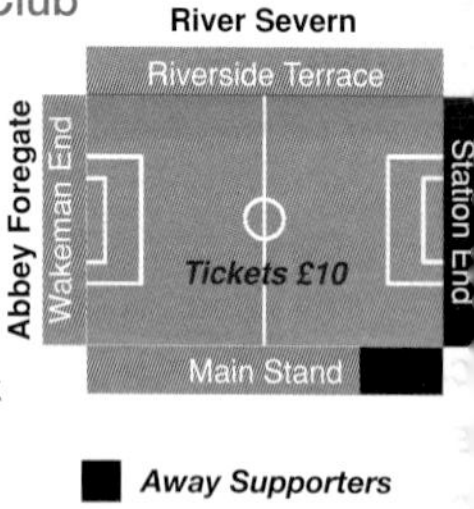

Address:
Gay Meadow
Shrewsbury
Shropshire
SY2 6AB

Switch Board: 01743 360111

Ticket Office: 01743 360111

Website: www.shrewsburytown.co.uk

Nickname: The Shrews

Year Formed: 1886

Record Attendance: 18,917 v Walsall Apr, 1961

Record Receipts: £80,610 v Arsenal Feb, 1991

Record League Victory: 7-0 v Swindon T May, 1955

Record Cup Victory: 11-2 v Marine Nov, 1995

Record Defeat: 1-8 v Norwich C Sept, 1952

Most Capped Player: Jimmy McLaughlin, Northern Ireland 5. Bernard McNally, Northern Ireland 5

Most League Appearances: Colin Griffin 406

Record Transfer Fee Received:
£500,000 for Dave Walton, Oct 1997

Record Transfer Fee Paid:
£100,000 for John Dungworth, Nov 1979

Capacity: 8,000   **Fanzine:** A Large Scotch

Away Capacity: 1,500 **Unofficial site:** www.stfc-terrace-talk.co.uk

Disabled places: 125

Last 5 Seasons:	Last 5 Managers:
1997: Div 2 - 22nd	Asa Hartford (90-91)
1998: Div 3 - 13th	John Bond (91-93)
1999: Div 3 - 15th	Fred Davies (94-97)
2000: Div 3 - 22nd	Jake King (97-99)
2001: Div 3 - 15th	Kevin Ratcliffe (99-Pre)

Shrewsbury Town Football Club

Travel:

Rail: Shrewsbury 08457 484950

Bus: National Coach Enquiries 0870 6082608

Car:

East:

Come off the M6 at Junction 10a and follow the M54 through Telford, the road then becomes the A5. When you get to the end of the A5 you will meet a roundabout. Take the first exit left and continue to the next roundabout where you should take the fourth exit which is signposted for the crematorium. Follow this road until you meet an Island with a large statue in the middle of it. Go straight across (3rd exit) and you will find yourself on the Abbey Foregate Road. Continue down the road and you will see a railway bridge ahead of you. The Gay Meadow is the first right after the bridge.

South:

Use the A49 and follow the signs for Shrewsbury town centre then at the end of Coleham Head turn right into Abbey Foregate.

North:

Use A49 or A53 and at the first island take the second exit, 5112 into Telford Way. At the next island take the 2nd exit then at the T- junction turn right into Abbey Foregate.

MY RATING

Date Visited: _____

Rating out of 10:

1 2 3 4 5 6 7 8 9 10

Note: _____

Shrewsbury Town Football Club

Honours:

Football League: Division 2: Best season: 8th, 1983-1984, 1984-1985. Division 3. Champions: 1978-1979, 1993-1994. Division 4. Runners-up: 1974-1975.

FA Cup: Best season: 6th rd, 1979, 1982.

Football League Cup: Semi-final: 1961.

Welsh Cup: Winners: 1891, 1938, 1977, 1979, 1984, 1985. Runners-up: 1931, 1948, 1980.

Auto Windscreens Shield: Runners-up: 1996.

Southampton Football Club

Address:
St. Mary's Stadium
Brittania Road
Southampton, SO14 5FP
Switch Board: 0870 2200000
Ticket Office: 0870 7771000
Website: www.saintsfc.co.uk
Nickname: The Saints
Year Formed: 1885
Record Attendance: 31,044 v Manchester U Oct, 1969
Record Receipts: £277,863 v Tranmere R Feb, 2001
Record league Victory: 9-3 v Wolverhampton W Sep, 1965
Record Cup Victory: 7-1 v Ipswich T Jan, 1961. v Everton Nov, 1971.
Record Defeat: 0-8 v Tottenham H Mar, 1936
Most Capped Player: Peter Shilton, England 49
Most League Appearances: Terry Paine, 713
Record Transfer Fee Received:
8,100,000 for Dean Richards, Sep 2001
Record Transfer Fee Paid:
4,000,000 for Rory Delap, Jul 2001
Capacity: 32,000   **Fanzine:** The Beautiful South
Away Capacity: 6,000 **Unofficial site:** www.saintsforever.com
Disabled places: Varies

Last 5 Seasons:	Last 5 Managers:
1997: Prem - 16th	Dave Merrington (95-96)
1998: Prem - 12th	Graeme Souness (96-97)
1999: Prem - 17th	Dave Jones (97-00)
2000: Prem - 15th	Glenn Hoddle (00-01)
2001: Prem - 10th	Stuart Gray (01-Pre)

Southampton Football Club

Travel:

Rail: Southampton Central 08457 484950

Bus: National Coach Enquiries 0870 6082608

Car:

From all Directions:

Follow the M3 until it reaches the end of the motorway and come off at the exit signposted M27 West, Southampton Docks. Travel along this road for 3/4 of a mile before bearing left at the fork on the A33 which is signposted Southampton. At the second roundabout take the first exit into Bassett Avenue A33. As you progress along this road the name changes twice firstly to the Avenue and then Dorset Street. At the roundabout take the second exit (still Dorset Street) and then take the second right into Saint Mary's Kingsway. Take the first right into Chapel Street and then first left into Melbourne Street. The Ground is directly ahead of you

MY RATING

Date Visited: _____

Rating out of 10:

1 2 3 4 5 6 7 8 9 10

Note: _____

Southampton Football Club

Honours:

Football League: Division 1. Runners-up: 1983-1984. **Division 2. Runners-up:** 1965-1966, 1977-1978. **Division 3 (S). Champions:** 1921-1922. **Runners-up:** 1920-1921. **Division 3. Champions:** 1959-1960.

FA Cup: Winners: 1976. **Runners-up:** 1900, 1902.

Football League Cup: Runners-up: 1979.

Zenith Data Systems Cup: Runners-up: 1992.

European Competitions:

European Fairs Cup: 1969-1970.

UEFA Cup: 1971-1972, 1981-1982, 1982-1983, 1984-1985.

European Cup-Winners' Cup: 1976-1977.

Southend Football Club

Address:
Roots Hall Football Ground
Victoria Avenue
Southend-on-Sea
SS2 6NQ

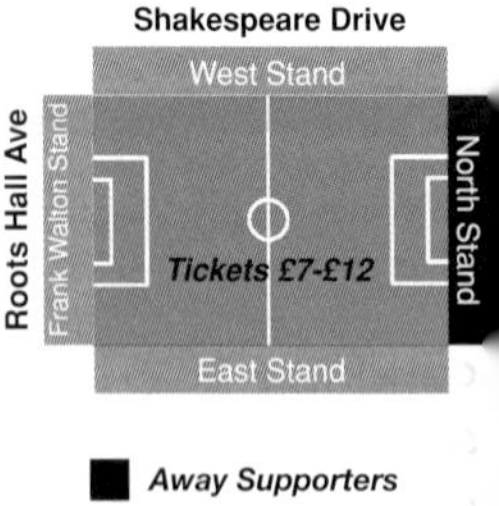

Switch Board: 01702 304050

Ticket Office: 01702 304090

Website: www.southendunited.co.uk

Nickname: The Shrimpers

Year Formed: 1906

Record Attendance: 31,090 v Liverpool Jan, 1979

Record Receipts: £83,999 v West Ham U Apr, 1993

Record League Victory: 9-2 v Newport Co Sep, 1936

Record Cup Victory: 10-1 v Golders Green Nov, 1934. v Brentwoo
Dec, 1968. v Aldershot Nov, 1990

Record Defeat: 1-9 v Brighton & HA Nov, 1965

Most Capped Player: George Mackenzie, 9 Eire

Most League Appearances: Sandy Anderson, 452

Record Transfer Fee Received:
£3,570,000 for Stan Collymore, Jun 1993

Record Transfer Fee Paid:
£750,000 for Stan Collymore, Nov 1992

Capacity: 12,392   **Fanzine:** What's the Story

Away Capacity: 3,500 **Unofficial site:** www.shrimperzone.com

Disabled places: 20

Shakespeare Drive — West Stand — Roots Hall Ave — Frank Walton Stand — Tickets £7-£12 — East Stand — North Stand

Away Supporters

Last 5 Seasons:	Last 5 Managers:
1997: Div 1 - 24th	Steve Thompson (95)
1998: Div 2 - 24th	Ronnie Whelan (95-97)
1999: Div 3 - 18th	Alvin Martin (97-99)
2000: Div 3 - 16th	Alan Little (99-00)
2001: Div 3 - 11th	David Webb (00-Pre)

Southend United Football Club

Travel:

Rail: Prittlewell 08457 484950

Bus: National Coach Enquiries 0870 6082608

Car:

South, East:

From the M25 take junction 29 and follow the A127 to the town centre passing Tesco's and the Bell pub. Having past the pub turn right at the next roundabout (3rd turning) along Victoria Avenue towards the town centre. As you climb the next hill you will see the ground on the right.

North:

Follow the A130 until you come to the A127. Turn left onto the A127 and then as South/East.

Honours:

Football League: Division 1. Best season: 13th, 1994-1995. Division 3. Runners-up: 1990-1991. Division 4. Champions: 1980-1981. Runners-up: 1971-1972, 1977-1978.

FA Cup: Best season: Old 3rd rd, 1921, 5th rd, 1926, 1952, 1976, 1993.

Football League Cup: Never past 3rd rd.

MY RATING

Date Visited: _____

Rating out of 10:

1 2 3 4 5 6 7 8 9 10

Note: _____

Stockport County Football Club

Address:
Edgeley Park
Hardcastle Road
Stockport
Cheshire, SK3 9DD
Switch Board: 0161 2868888
Ticket Office: 0161 2868888
Website: www.stockportcounty.com
Nickname: The Hatters
Year Formed: 1883
Record Attendance: 27,833 v Liverpool Feb, 1950
Record Receipts: £181,449 v Middlesbrough Feb, 1997
Record League Victory: 13-0 v Halifax Jan, 1934
Record Cup Victory: 5-0 v Lincoln Nov, 1995
Record Defeat: 1-8 v Chesterfield Apr, 1902
Most Capped Player: Martin Nash, Canada 8
Most League Appearances: Andy Thorpe, 489
Record Transfer Fee Received:
£1,600,000 for Alun Armstrong, Feb 1998
Record Transfer Fee Paid:
£800,000 for Ian Moore, Jul 1998
Capacity: 11,541   **Fanzine:** IO County
Away Capacity: 3,800 Unofficial site: stockportcounty2000.co.uk
Disabled places: 12

Last 5 Seasons:	Last 5 Managers:
1997: Div 2 - 2nd	Asa Hartford (87-89)
1998: Div 1 - 8th	Danny Bergara (89-95)
1999: Div 1 - 16th	Dave Jones (95-97)
2000: Div 1 - 17th	Gary Megson (97-99)
2001: Div 1 - 19th	Andy Kilner (99-Pre)

Stockport County Football Club

Travel:

Rail: Stockport Edgeley 08457 484950

Bus: National Coach Enquiries 0870 6082608

Car:

South:

Exit the M6 at junction 19 (signposted 'Manchester Airport, Stockport A55, M56 East') and at the roundabout turn right onto the A556. After 4 miles turn right onto the M56 (signposted Manchester M56). Follow the M56 bearing right as it joins the M60 (signposted Stockport M60, Sheffield M67) Exit the M60 at junction 1 (signposted 'Stockport Town Centre'). At the roundabout, follow signs to 'Cheadle A560' also 'Stockport County FC' into Hollywood Way. Go straight on at the first set of traffic lights and then turn right at the next set (signposted 'Cheadle A560, Stockport County FC') onto the A560. After 1.1 miles, turn onto the B5465 Edgeley Road. After approximately 1 mile turn right into Dale Street at the traffic lights and take the second left into Hardcastle Road for the stadium.

North:

Follow the M62 onto the M60 and continue South. Exit the M60 at junction 1 (signposted 'Stockport Town Centre) and then follow directions as South.

MY RATING

Date Visited: _____

Rating out of 10:

1 2 3 4 5 6 7 8 9 10

Note: _____

Stockport County Football Club

Honours:

Football League: Division 1: Best season: 8th, 1997-1998.
Division 2. Runners-up: 1996-1997. **Division 3 (N). Champions:** 1921-1922, 1936-1937. **Runners-up:** 1928-1929, 1929-1930.
Division 4. Champions: 1966-1967. **Runners-up:** 1990-1991.

FA Cup: Best season: 5th rd, 1935, 1950.

Football League Cup: Semi-final: 1997.

Autoglass Trophy: Runners-up: 1992, 1993.

Stoke City Football Club

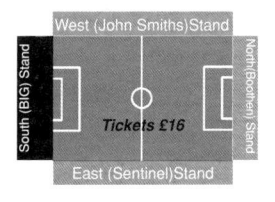

Address:
Britannia Stadium
Stanley Matthews Way
Stoke-on-Trent, ST4 4EG
Switch Board: 01782 592222
Ticket Office: 01782 592222
Website: www.stokecityfc.com
Nickname: The Potters
Year Formed: 1863
Record Attendance: 51,380 v Arsenal Mar, 1937
Record Receipts: £336,000 v Liverpool Nov, 2000
Record League Victory: 10-3 v WBA Feb, 1937
Record Cup Victory: 7-1 v Burnley Feb, 1896
Record Defeat: 0-10 v Preston Sep, 1889
Most Capped Player: Gordon Banks, England 36
Most League Appearances: Eric Skeels, 506
Record Transfer Fee Received:
£2,750,000 for Mike Sheron, Jul 1997
Record Transfer Fee Paid:
£600,000 for Brnynjar Gunnarsson, Dec 1999
Capacity: 28,384   **Fanzine:** The Oatcake
Away Capacity: 4,964 **Unofficial site:** www.oatcake.co.uk
Disabled places: 160

Last 5 Seasons:	Last 5 Managers:
1997: Div 1 - 12th	Chic Bates (97-98)
1998: Div 1 - 23rd	Chris Kamara (98)
1999: Div 2 - 8th	Brian Little (98-99)
2000: Div 2 - 6th	Gary Megson (99)
2001: Div 2 - 5th	Gudjon Thordarson (99-Pre)

Stoke City Football Club

Travel:

Rail: Stoke on Trent
08457 484950

Bus: National Coach
Enquiries 0870 6082608

Car:

North/South/West:

Take the M6 to junction 15 and come off onto the A500 to Stoke-on-Trent then the A50 to Derby/Uttoxeter (the Britannia Stadium is signposted and visible on the sky-line to the right). Once on the A50 drive past the stadium on the right to the first exit and come back down the westbound carriageway of the A50.

East:

Take the A50 all the way to Stoke-on-Trent and you will eventually see the stadium on the left.

Honours:

Football League: Division 1: Best season: 4th, 1935-1936, 1946-1947. Division 2. Champions: 1932-1933, 1962-1963, 1992-1993. Runners-up: 1921-1922. Promoted: 1978-1979 (3rd). Division (N). Champions: 1926-1927.

FA Cup: Semi-finals: 1899, 1971, 1972. Football League Cup: Winners: 1972. Autoglass Trophy: Winners: 1992. Auto Windscreens Shield: Winners: 2000.

European Competitions: UEFA Cup: 1972-1973, 1974-1975.

MY RATING

Date Visited: _____

Rating out of 10:
1 2 3 4 5 6 7 8 9 10

Note: _____

Sunderland Football Club

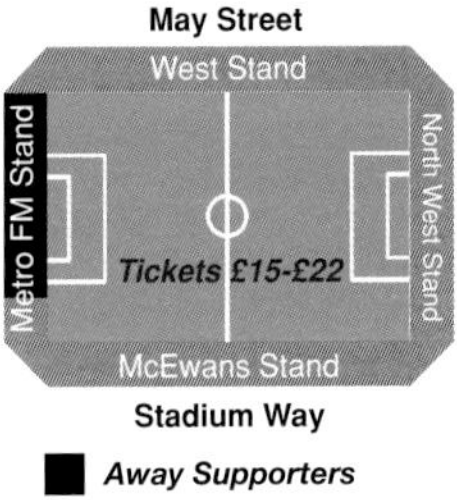

Address:
The Stadium of Light
Tyne & Wear
Sunderland, SR5 1SU

Switch Board: 0191 5515000

Ticket Office: 0191 5515151

Website: www.safc.com

Nickname: The Black Cats

Year Formed: 1879

Record Attendance: 48,285 v Leeds U Mar, 2001 (Stadium of Light). 75,118 v Derby Mar, 1933 (Roker Park).

Record Receipts: £605,310 v Sheffield U May, 1998

Record League Victory: 9-1 v Newcastle U Dec, 1908

Record Cup Victory: 11-1 v Fairfield Feb, 1895

Record Defeat: 0-8 v Sheff Wed Dec, 1911. v West Ham Oct, 1968. v Watford Sep, 1982.

Most Capped Player: Charlie Hurley, Republic of Ireland 38

Most League Appearances: Jim Montgomery, 537

Record Transfer Fee Received:
£5,600,000 for Michael Bridges, Jul 1999

Record Transfer Fee Paid:
£4,500,000 for Emerson Thome, Sep 2000

Capacity: 48,300   **Fanzine:** A Love Supreme

Away Capacity: 3,000 **Unofficial site:** www.readytogo.net

Disabled places: 180

Last 5 Seasons:	Last 5 Managers:
1997: Prem - 18th	Denis Smith (87-91)
1998: Div 1 - 3rd	Malcolm Crosby (92-93)
1999: Div 1 - 1st	Terry Butcher (93)
2000: Prem - 7th	Mick Buxton (93-95)
2001: Prem - 7th	Peter Reid (95-Pre)

Sunderland Football Club

Travel:

Rail: Sunderland 08457 484950

Bus: National Coach Enquiries 0870 6082608

Car:

From all Directions:

Exit the A1M at junction 64 and pick up the A195 signposted to Washington. Follow the Western Highway and after 1.5 miles you will come to a roundabout. Follow signs for Sunderland A1231 on the Washington Highway. Take the second exit for the A1231 and then head for the city centre going for 4.5 miles (following signs for the B1289). Once on the B1289 (Queens Road) turn right at the roundabout and straight over at the next roundabout and you will see the Stadium of Light.

MY RATING

Date Visited: _____

Rating out of 10:
1 2 3 4 5 6 7 8 9 10

Note: _____

Sunderland Football Club

Honours:

Football League: Division 1. Champions: 1891-1892, 1892-1893, 1894-1895, 1901-1902, 1912-1913, 1935-1936, 1995-1996, 1998-1999. Runners-up: 1893-1894, 1897-1898, 1900-1901, 1922-1923, 1934-1935. Division 2. Champions: 1975-1976. Runners-up: 1963-1964, 1979-1980. Division 3. Champions: 1987-1988.

FA Cup: Winners: 1937, 1973. Runners-up: 1913, 1992.

Football League Cup: Runners-up: 1985.

European Competitions:

European Cup-Winners' Cup: 1973-1974.

Swansea City Football Club

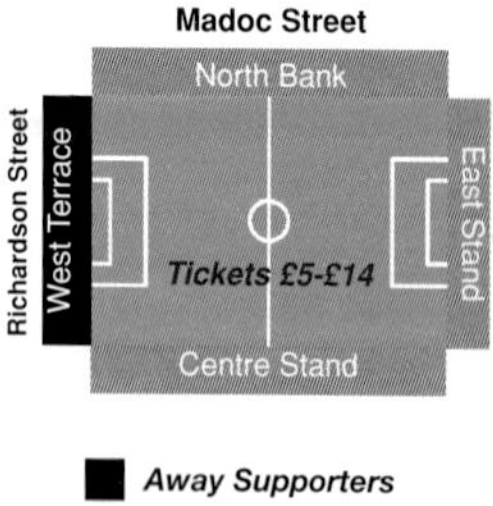

Address:
Vetch Field
Swansea
SA1 3SU

Switch Board: 01792 474114
Ticket Office: 01792 474114
Website: www.swanseacity.net
Nickname: The Swans
Year Formed: 1912
Record Attendance: 32,796 v Arsenal Feb, 1968
Record Receipts: £36,477.42 v Liverpool Sep, 1982
Record League Victory: 8-0 v Hartlepool U Apr, 1978
Record Cup Victory: 12-0 v Sliema W Sept, 1982
Record Defeat: 0-8 v Liverpool Jan, 1990. v Monaco Oct,1991
Most Capped Player: Ivor Allchurch, Wales 42
Most League Appearances: Wilfred Milne, 585
Record Transfer Fee Received:
£400,000 for Steve Torpey, Aug 1997
Record Transfer Fee Paid:
£340,000 for Colin Irwin, Aug 1981
Capacity: 10,402   **Fanzine:** Jackplug
Away Capacity: 2,000 Unofficial site: www.scfc.co.uk
Disabled places: 15

Last 5 Seasons:	Last 5 Managers:
1997: Div 3 - 5th	Kevin Cullis (96)
1998: Div 3 - 20th	Jan Molby (96-97)
1999: Div 3 - 7th	Micky Adams (97)
2000: Div 3 - 1st	Alan Cork (97-98)
2001: Div 2 - 23rd	John Hollins (98-Pre)

Swansea City Football Club

Travel:

Rail: Swansea 08457 484950

Bus: National Coach Enquiries 0870 6082608

Car:

North/East:

From the M4, come off at junction 42 onto the A483 towards Swansea. Continue along the sea front and look out for the A4067 (Oystermouth). Once you have exited onto the A4067, follow signs towards Mumbles. You will see the floodlights in the distance, continue until you come to the prison, turn right and you will see the ground.

West:

Follow the M4 to junction 45 and then take the A4067 towards the city centre. Follow the A4067 and continue as North.

MY RATING

Date Visited: _____

Rating out of 10:
1 2 3 4 5 6 7 8 9 10

Note: _____

Swansea City Football Club

Honours:

Football League: Division 1: Best season: 6th, 1981-1982. Division 2. Promoted 1980-1981 (3rd). Division 3 (S). Champions: 1924-1925, 1948-1949. Division 3. Champions: 1999-2000. Promoted 1978-1979 (3rd). Division 4. Promoted 1969-1970 (3rd), 1977-1978 (3rd), 1987-1988 (play-offs).

FA Cup: Semi-finals: 1926, 1964.

Football League Cup: Best season: 4th rd, 1965, 1977.

Welsh Cup: Winners: 9 times: Runners-up: 8 times.

Autoglass Trophy: Winners: 1994.

European Competitions:

European Cup-Winners' Cup: 1961-1962, 1966-1967, 1981-1982, 1982-1983, 1983-1984, 1989-1990, 1991-1992.

Swindon Town Football Club

Address:
County Ground
County Road
Swindon
Wiltshire, SN1 2ED
Switch Board: 01793 333700
Ticket Office: 01793 333777
Website: www.swindontownfc.co.uk
Nickname: The Robins
Year Formed: 1881
Record Attendance: 32,000 v Arsenal Jan, 1972
Record Receipts: £149,371 v Bolton W Feb, 1995
Record League Victory: 9-1 v Luton Aug, 1920
Record Cup Victory: 10-1 v Farnham U Nov, 1925
Record Defeat: 1-10 v Manchester City Jan, 1930
Most Capped Player: Rod Thomas, Wales 30
Most League Appearances: John Trollope, 770
Record Transfer Fee Received:
£1,500,000 for Kevin Horlock, Jan 1997
Record Transfer Fee Paid:
£800,000 for Joey Beauchamp, Aug 1994
Capacity: 15,728   **Fanzine:** The Magic Roundabout
Away Capacity: 3,000 **Unofficial site:** www.myonlyswindon.com
Disabled places: 49

Last 5 Seasons:	Last 5 Managers:
1997: Div 1 - 19th	John Gorman (93-94)
1998: Div 1 - 18th	Steve McMahon (94-99)
1999: Div 1 - 17th	Jimmy Quinn (99-00)
2000: Div 1 - 24th	Colin Todd (00)
2001: Div 2 - 20th	Andy King (00-Pre)

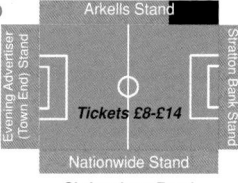

Tickets £8-£14

Shrivenham Road

Away Supporters

Swindon Town Football Club

Travel:

Rail: Swindon 08457 484950

Bus: National Coach Enquiries 0870 6082608

Car: South, East and West: Leave the M4 at junction 15. When you come to the first roundabout (called the Commonhead) turn left onto the A4529 Marlborough road. Take the 2nd exit at the next roundabout onto Queens Drive. At the next set of roundabouts take the 3rd exit onto County Road and the entrance to the ground is first on the right.

North: From the A419, follow the Cricklade Road down the hill. The road will then become Cirencester Way. At the transfer bridges roundabouts, go left at the first roundabout and then straight over at the second. The football ground is on the left after the mini roundabout.

MY RATING

Date Visited: _____

Rating out of 10:

1 2 3 4 5 6 7 8 9 10

Note: _____

Honours:

FA Premier League: Best season: 22nd, 1993-1994.

Football League: Division 2. Champions 1995-1996. Division 3. Runners-up: 1962-1963, 1968-1969. Division 4. Champions: 1985-1986.

FA Cup: Semi-finals: 1910, 1912. Football League Cup: Winners 1969. Anglo-Italian Cup: Winners: 1970.

Torquay United Football Club

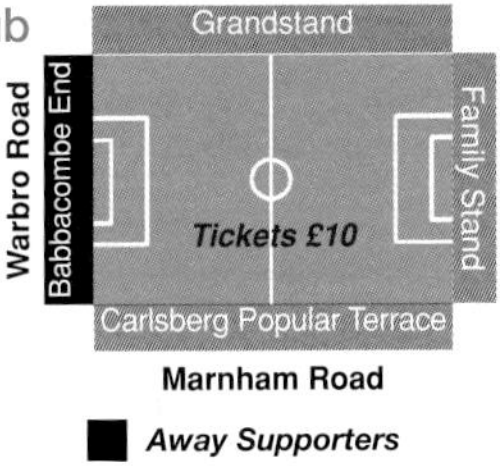

Address:
Plainmoor Ground
Torquay
Devon, TQ1 3PS
Switch Board: 01803 328666
Ticket Office: 01803 328666
Website: www.torquayunited.com
Nickname: The Gulls
Year Formed: 1899
Record Attendance: 21,908 v Huddersfield T Jan, 1955
Record Receipts: £30,834 v Plymouth A Mar, 2000
Record League Victory: 9-0 v Swindon T Mar, 1952
Record Cup Victory: 7-1 v Northampton T Nov, 1959
Record Defeat: 2-10 v Fulham Sep, 1931
Most Capped Player: Rodney Jack, St Vincent
Most League Appearances: Dennis Lewis, 443
Record Transfer Fee Received:
£500,000 for Rodney Jack, Jul 1998
Record Transfer Fee Paid:
£70,000 for Eifion Williams, Mar 1999
Capacity: 6,283 **Fanzine:** Bambers Right Foot
Away Capacity: 1,515 **Unofficial site:** www.torquayunited.net
Disabled places: 15

Last 5 Seasons:	Last 5 Managers:
1997: Div 3 - 21st	Paul Compton (92-93)
1998: Div 3 - 5th	Don O'Riordan (93-95)
1999: Div 3 - 20th	Eddie May (95-96)
2000: Div 3 - 9th	Kevin Hodges (96-98)
2001: Div 3 - 21st	Wes Saunders (98-Pre)

Torquay United Football Club

Travel:

Rail: Torre 08457 484950

Bus: National Coach Enquiries: 0870 6082608

Car:

North/East: At the end of the M5 continue onto the A38 and then then turn left onto the A380. On reaching Kingskerwell, take the first exit at the roundabout and after one mile turn left onto the A3022 (signposted Babbacombe). After 1 mile turn left into Westhill Road. This then becomes Warbo Road and you will see the ground 200 yards on the right hand side.

West: Follow the A380 into Torquay town centre. On Union Street turn right into Lymington Road. As you pass the coach station turn right into Upton Hill and then 300 Meters later go left into St Marychurch Road. At the next cross roads, head into Warbo Road and the ground is on your right.

MY RATING

Date Visited: _____

Rating out of 10:

1 2 3 4 5 6 7 8 9 10

Note: _____

Honours:

Football League: Division 3. Best season: 4th, 1967-1968. Division 3 (S). Runners-up: 1956-1957. Division 4. Promoted 1959-1960 (3rd), 1965-1966 (3rd), 1990-1991 (play-offs).

FA Cup: Best season: 4th rd, 1949, 1955, 1971, 1983, 1990.

Football League Cup: Never past 3rd round.

Sherpa Van Trophy: Runners-up: 1989.

Tottenham Hotspur Football Club

Address:
White Hart Lane
Bill Nicholson Way
748 High Road
Tottenham
London, N17 0AP

Switch Board: 020 8365 5000
Ticket Office: 08700 112222
Website: www.spurs.co.uk

Nickname: Spurs
Year Formed: 1882
Record Attendance: 75,038 v Sunderland Mar, 1938
Record Receipts: £336,702 v Manchester U Sep, 1991
Record League Victory: 9-0 v Bristol R Oct, 1977
Record Cup Victory: 13-2 v Crewe Alex Feb, 1960
Record Defeat: 0-8 v Cologne Jul, 1995
Most Capped Player: Pat Jennings, Northern Ireland 74
Most League Appearances: Steve Perryman, 655
Record Transfer Fee Received:
£5,500,000 for Paul Gascoigne, May 1992
Record Transfer Fee Paid:
£11,000,000 for Sergei Rebrov, May 2000
Capacity: 36,236   **Fanzine:** One Flew Over Seaman's Head
Away Capacity: 3,000 **Unofficial site:** www.glory-glory.net
Disabled places: 43

High Road — West Stand — South Stand — North Stand — East Stand — Worcester Ave
Tickets £24-£46
■ *Away Supporters*

Last 5 Seasons:	Last 5 Managers:
1997: Prem - 10th	Ossie Ardiles (93-94)
1998: Prem - 14th	Gerry Francis (94-97)
1999: Prem - 11th	Christian Gross (97-98)
2000: Prem - 10th	George Graham (98-01)
2001: Prem - 12th	Glenn Hoddle (01-Pre)

Tottenham Hotspur Football Club

Travel:

Rail: White Hart lane
08457 484950

Tube: Seven Sisters, Victoria Line

Bus: National Coach Enquiries 0870 6082608

Car:

North:

From the M1 come off at junction 2/3 onto the A1. When you join the A406 head Eastbound for 7 miles. At the Edmonton traffic lights turn right onto the A1010 (Fore Street). Travel along Fore Street for 1 mile and the ground is on the left.

West:

Continue along the M4 until you get to junction 1. Head for the A406 North circular and after 13 miles you will reach the Edmonton traffic lights. Then travel as North.

East:

Follow the M11 to junction 4 and then come off onto the A406 heading Westbound for 6 miles until you reach the Edmonton traffic lights. Then travel as North.

MY RATING

Date Visited: _____

Rating out of 10:

1 2 3 4 5 6 7 8 9 10

Note: _____

Tottenham Hotspur Football Club

Honours:

Football League: Division 1. Champions: 1950-1951, 1960-1961. Runners-up: 1921-1922, 1951-1952, 1956-1957, 1962-1963. **Division 2. Champions:** 1919-1920, 1949-1950. Runners-up: 1908-1909, 1932-1933. Promoted: 1977-1978 (3rd).

FA Cup: Winners: 1901 (as non League club), 1921, 1961, 1962, 1967, 1981, 1982, 1991. Runners-up: 1987.

Football League Cup: Winners: 1971, 1973, 1999. Runners-up: 1982.

European Competitions:

European Cup: 1961-1962.

European Cup-Winners' Cup: 1962-1963 (winners), 1963-1964, 1967-1968, 1981-1982, 1982-1983, 1991-1992.

UEFA Cup: 1971-1972 (winners), 1972-1973, 1973-1974 (runners-up), 1983-1984 (winners), 1984-1985, 1999-2000.

Tranmere Rovers Football Club

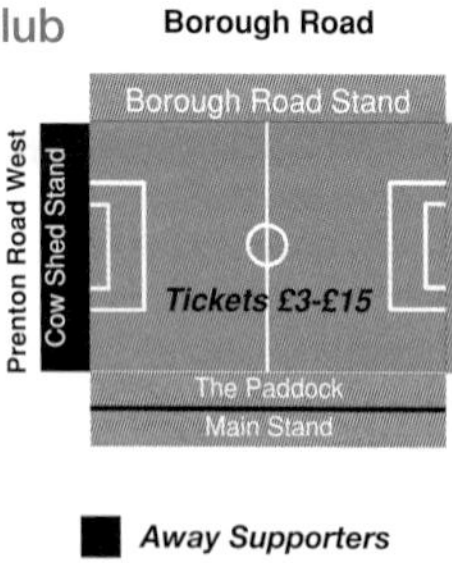

Borough Road

Address:
Prenton Park
Prenton Road West
Wirral, CH42 9PY
Switch Board: 0151 6084194
Ticket Office: 0151 6093322
Website: www.tranmererovers.co.uk
Nickname: Rovers
Year Formed: 1884
Record Attendance:
 24,424 v Stoke C Feb, 1972
Record Receipts: £268,946 v Liverpool Mar, 2001
Record League Victory: 13-4 v Oldham Ath Dec, 1935
Record Cup Victory: 13-0 v Oswestry U Oct, 1914
Record Defeat: 1-9 v Tottenham H Jan, 1953
Most Capped Player: John Aldridge, Republic of Ireland 30
Most League Appearances: Harold Bell, 595
Record Transfer Fee Received:
£3,300,000 for Steve Simonsen, Sep 1998
Record Transfer Fee Paid:
£450,000 for Shaun Teale, Aug 1995
Capacity: 16,587   **Fanzine:** Give Us An R
Away Capacity: 2,500
Unofficial site: www.unofficialtranmererovers.co.uk
Disabled places: 38

Last 5 Seasons:	Last 5 Managers:
1997: Div 1 - 11th	Frank Worthington (85-87)
1998: Div 1 - 14th	Ronnie Moore (87)
1999: Div 1 - 15th	John King (87-96)
2000: Div 1 - 13th	John Aldridge (96-01)
2001: Div 1 - 24th	Dave Watson (01-Pre)

Tranmere Rovers Football Club

Travel:

Rail: Birkenhead Central
08457 484950

Bus: National Coach
Enquiries 0870 6082608

Car:

From North Mersey Tunnel (Wallasey):

Using the Mersey Tunnel (Wallasey) join the M53 and exit at junction 3. At the roundabout leave at the first exit (A552). Continue on this road passing the Swan pub, Kwik Save and Sainsbury's. At the Halfway House pub, turn right, then first left into Woodchurch lane. Prenton Park is at the bottom of Woodchurch Lane on Prenton Road West.

From North Mersey Tunnel (Birkenhead):

Leave the tunnel and take the flyover on the right hand side. The flyover joins Borough Road, near the Pyramids Shopping Centre. Continue along Borough Road passing two Shell Garages (on left) and the College (on right). Prenton Park can be seen at the next set of traffic lights.

South:

Using the M53 leave at junction 4. At the roundabout take the the 4th exit B5151 and continue until you reach the double roundabout. Prenton Park is signposted from here.

MY RATING

Date Visited: _____

Rating out of 10:

1 2 3 4 5 6 7 8 9 10

Note: _____
_____
_____
_____

Tranmere Rovers Football Club

Honours:

Football League: Division 1. Best season: 4th, 1992-1993. Promoted from Division 3. 1990-1991 (play-offs). Division 3 (N). Champions: 1937-1938. Promotion to 3rd Division: 1966-1967, 1975-1976. Division 4. Runners-up: 1988-1989.

FA Cup: Best season: 6th rd, 2000, 2001.

Football League Cup: Runners-up: 2000.

Welsh Cup: Winners: 1935. Runners-up: 1934.

Leyland Daf Cup: Winners: 1990. Runners-up: 1991

Walsall Football Club

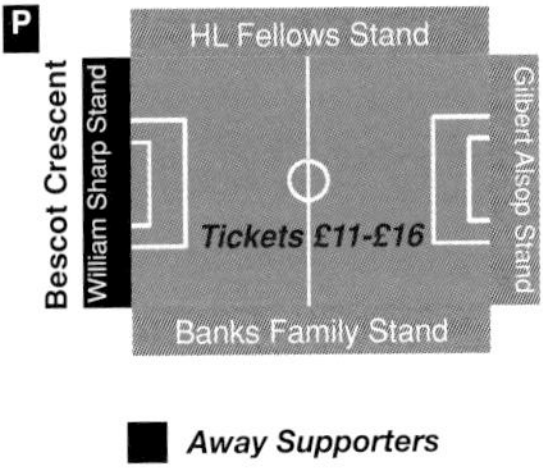

Address:
Bescot Stadium
Bescot Crescent
Walsall, WS1 4SA
Switch Board: 01922 622791
Ticket Office: 01922 651416
Website: www.saddlers.co.uk
Nickname: The Saddlers
Year Formed: 1888
Record Attendance: 10,628 England v Switzerland May, 1991
Record Receipts: £98,828 v Leeds U Jan, 1995
Record League Victory: 10-0 v Darwen Mar, 1899
Record Cup Victory: 7-0 v Macclesfield T Dec, 1997
Record Defeat: 0-12 v Small Heath Dec, 1892. v Darwen Dec, 1896.
Most Capped Player: Mick Kearns, Republic of Ireland 15
Most League Appearances: Colin Harrison, 467
Record Transfer Fee Received:
£600,000 for David Kelly, Jul 1988
Record Transfer Fee Paid:
£175,000 for Alan Buckley, Jun 1979
Capacity: 9,000   **Fanzine:** Blazing Saddlers
Away Capacity: 1,915 **Unofficial site:** www.steveroy.com/walsall
Disabled places: 30

Tickets £11-£16

Away Supporters

Last 5 Seasons:	Last 5 Managers:
1997: Div 2 - 12th	John Barnwell (89-90)
1998: Div 2 - 19th	Kenny Hibbitt (90-94)
1999: Div 2 - 2nd	Chris Nicholl (94-97)
2000: Div 1 - 22nd	Jan Sorensen (97-98)
2001: Div 2 - 4th	Ray Graydon (98-Pre)

Walsall Football Club

Travel:

Rail: Bescot 08457 484950

Bus: National Coach Enquiries 0870 6082608

Car: North, South, West: Leave the M6 at junction 9. Take the A461 (Bescot Road) towards Walsall (you will see signs for Bescot stadium from here). At the traffic lights stay in the right hand lane and follow the A4148 (Wallows Lane) through a second set of traffic lights (you will notice that the road name has changed to Broadway West). At the third set of traffic lights turn right into Bescot Crescent. Follow the road around and the second turning on the left is the entrance to Bescot Stadium.

East: When approaching Walsall from the A461 take the first exit A4146 at the Arboretum Island (Broadway North). Continue across the next three islands (A4148 Broadway North). At the fourth set of traffic lights turn left into Bescot Crescent. Follow the road around and the second turning on the left is the entrance to Bescot Stadium.

Honours: Football League: Division 2. Runners-up: 1998-1999. Promoted to Division 1 2000-2001. Division 3. Runners-up: 1960-1961, 1994-1995. Division 4. Champions: 1959-1960. Runners-up: 1979-1980. FA Cup: Best season, 5th rd, 1939, 1975, 1978, 1987 and last 16 1889. Football League Cup: Semi final: 1984.

MY RATING

Date Visited: _____

Rating out of 10:
1 2 3 4 5 6 7 8 9 10

Note: _____

Watford Football Club

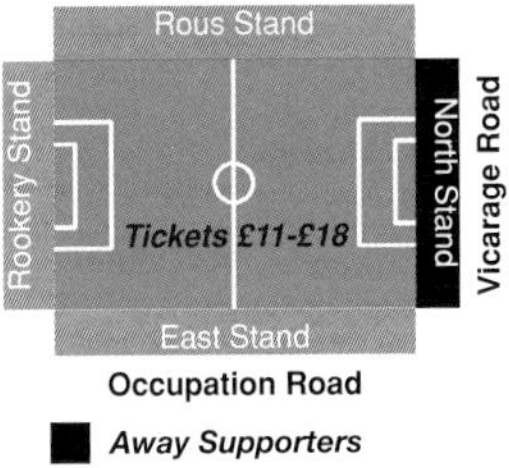

Address:
Vicarage Road Stadium
Vicarage Road
Watford, WD1 8ER
Switch Board: 01923 496000
Ticket Office: 01923 400010
Website: www.watfordfc.com
Nickname: The Hornets
Year Formed: 1881
Record Attendance: 34,099 v Manchester U Feb, 1969
Record Receipts: £440,349 v Chelsea Sep, 1999
Record League Victory: 8-0 v Sunderland Sep, 1982
Record Cup Victory: 10-1 v Lowestoft T Nov, 1926
Record Defeat: 0-10 v Wolverhampton W Jan, 1912
Most Capped Player: John Barnes, England 31. Kenny Jacket, Wales 31
Most League Appearances: Luther Blissett, 415
Record Transfer Fee Received:
2,300,000 for Paul Furlong, May 1994
Record Transfer Fee Paid:
3,250,000 for Allan Nielson, Aug 2000
Capacity: 20,800 **Fanzine:** CYHSYF
Away Capacity: 4,000 **Unofficial site:** www.bsad.org
Disabled places: 40

Tickets £11-£18

Away Supporters

Last 5 Seasons:	Last 5 Managers:
1997: Div 2 - 13th	Steve Perryman (90-93)
1998: Div 2 - 1st	Glenn Roeder (93-96)
1999: Div 1 - 5th	Kenny Jackett (96-97)
2000: Prem - 20th	Graham Taylor (97-01)
2001: Div 1 - 9th	Gianluca Vialli (01-Pre)

Watford Football Club

Travel:

Rail: Watford Halt, Watford Junction 08457 484950

Bus: National Coach Enquiries 0870 6082608

Car:

North: M1, J5 exit and at roundabout take A4008 signed Watford town centre. After 0.5 miles filter left again signed town centre, pass under railway bridge and take the 2nd exit (straight on) at the roundabout. Pass through the traffic lights and through 2 further sets of lights moving into the left hand lane of the ring road. After passing a mosque on your right then filter left after a further set of lights passing signs for the hospital. You are now in Vicarage Road. Follow the course of traffic and signs for West Watford and the hospital. After joining the small one way loop filter go left into Vicarage Road again, the ground is 250 yds on your left.

West: Exit the M25 at J19, travel 2 miles on the motorway link road to Hunton Bridge roundabout, here turn right to the A41 signed Watford, follow this road through the traffic lights for 3 miles until West Herts College appears on the right. At the roundabout shortly afterwards go straight on and at the 2nd roundabout, turn right into Rickmansworth Road. Take the 2nd left turn to Cassio Road and follow it through the traffic lights into Merton Road. Now follow signs fo the hospital forming a turn and then joining the one way loop, then as North.

MY RATING

Date Visited: _____

Rating out of 10:

1 2 3 4 5 6 7 8 9 10

Note: _____

Watford Football Club

Honours:

Football League: Division 1. Runners-up: 1982-1983, promoted from Division 1. 1998-1999 (play-offs). Division 2. Champions: 1997-1998. Runners-up: 1981-1982. Division 3. Champions: 1968-1969. Runners-up: 1978-1979. Division 4. Champions: 1977-1978. Promoted: 1959-1960 (4th).

FA Cup: Runners-up: 1984.

Football League Cup: Semi-final: 1979.

European Competitions:

UEFA Cup: 1983-1984.

West Bromwich Albion Football Club

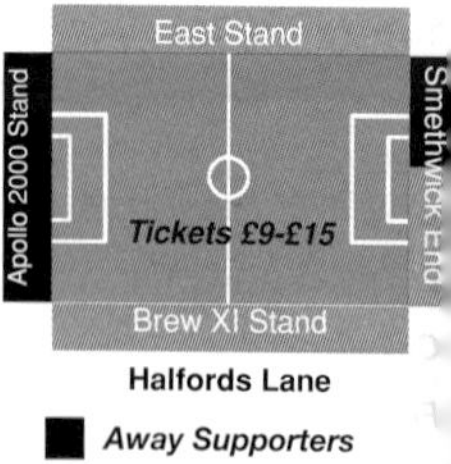

Address:
The Hawthorns
Halfords Lane
West Bromwich, B71 4LF
Switch Board: 0121 5258888
Ticket Office: 0121 5535472
Website: www.wba.co.uk
Nickname: The Baggies
Year Formed: 1878
Record Attendance: 64,815 v Arsenal Mar, 1937
Record Receipts: £270,000 v Nottingham F May, 1998
Record League Victory: 12-0 v Darwen Apr, 1892
Record Cup Victory: 10-1 v Chatham Mar, 1889
Record Defeat: 3-10 v Stoke C Feb, 1937
Most Capped Player: Stuart Williams, Wales 33
Most League Appearances: Tony Brown, 574
Record Transfer Fee Received:
£4,300,000 for Enzo Maresca, Jan 2000
Record Transfer Fee Paid:
£1,250,000 for Kevin Kilbane, Jun 1997
Capacity: 25,396 **Fanzine:** Grorty Dick
Away Capacity: 5,200 **Unofficial site:** www.wbaunofficial.com
Disabled places: 150

Last 5 Seasons:	Last 5 Managers:
1997: Div 1 - 16th	Alan Buckley (94-97)
1998: Div 1 - 10th	Ray Harford (97)
1999: Div 1 - 12th	Denis Smith (97-00)
2000: Div 1 - 21st	Brian Little (00)
2001: Div 1 - 6th	Gary Megson (00-Pre)

West Bromwich Albion Football Club

Travel:

Rail: Hawthorn's Halt
08457 484950

Bus: National Coach
Enquiries 0870 6082608

Car:

From all Directions:

Come off the M5 at junction 1 and take the A41 towards Birmingham along the Birmingham Road and signposted Handsworth. Simply continue along the A41 where you will pick up signs for the football ground.

Honours:

Football League: Division 1. Champions: 1919-1920. Runners-up: 1924-1925, 1953-1954. Division 2. Champions: 1901-1902, 1910-1911. Runners-up: 1930-1931, 1948-1949. Promoted to Division 1. 1975-1976 (3rd).

FA Cup: Winners: 1888, 1892, 1931, 1954, 1968. Runners-up: 1886, 1887, 1895, 1912, 1935.

Football League Cup: Winners: 1966. Runners-up: 1967, 1970.

European Competitions:

European Cup-Winners' Cup: 1968-1969.

European Fairs Cup: 1966-1967.

UEFA Cup: 1978-1979, 1979-1980, 1981-1982.

MY RATING

Date Visited: _____

Rating out of 10:

1 2 3 4 5 6 7 8 9 10

Note: _____

West Ham United Football Club

Address:
Boleyn Ground
Green Street
Upton Park
London, E13 9AZ

Switch Board: 020 8548 2748
Ticket Office: 020 8548 2700
Website: www.whufc.co.uk
Nickname: The Hammers
Year Formed: 1895

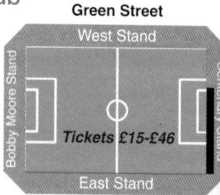

Green Street
West Stand
Bobby Moore Stand
Tickets £15-£46
East Stand
Priory Road

■ *Away Supporters*

Record Attendance: 42,322 v Tottenham H Oct, 1970
Record Receipts: £840,307 v Tottenham H Mar, 2001
Record League Victory: 8-0 v Rotherham U Mar, 1958. v Sunderland Oct, 1968.
Record Cup Victory: 10-0 v Bury Oct, 1983
Record Defeat: 2-8 v Blackburn R Dec, 1963
Most Capped Player: Bobby Moore, England 108
Most League Appearances: Billy Bonds, 663
Record Transfer Fee Received:
£18,000,000 for Rio Ferdinand, Nov 2000
Record Transfer Fee Paid:
£4,200,000 for Marc-Vivien Foe, Jan 1999
Capacity: 26,054   **Fanzine:** Over Land and Sea
Away Capacity: 2,225 **Unofficial site:** www.westhamonline.com
Disabled places: 116

Last 5 Seasons:	Last 5 Managers:
1997: Prem - 14th	John Lyall (74-89)
1998: Prem - 8th	Lou Macari (89-90)
1999: Prem - 5th	Billy Bonds (90-94)
2000: Prem - 9th	Harry Redknapp (94-01)
2001: Prem - 15th	Glenn Roeder (01-Pre)

West Ham United Football Club

Travel:

Rail: Barking 08457 484950

Tube: Upton Park (District Line)

Bus: National Coach Enquiries 0870 6082608

Car:

North:

From the M1 come of onto the A1 at junction 2/3. Head East along the A406 North Circular for 17 miles until you reach the junction with the A124. Turn right into Barking road (A124) and travel for 2 miles before going right into Green Street. Upton park is on the right.

East:

From the M11 come off at junction 4 and head Eastbound along the A406. Travel for 4 miles before reaching the junction with the A124. Then as North.

West:

From the M4 travel to the end of the motorway before turning onto the A406 Eastbound. Continue along the road for 26 miles until you reach the junction with the A124. Then as North.

MY RATING

Date Visited: _____

Rating out of 10:

1 2 3 4 5 6 7 8 9 10

Note: _____

West Ham United Football Club

Honours:

Football League: Division 1. Best season: 3rd, 1985-1986.
Division 2. Champions: 1957-1958, 1980-1981. Runners-up: 1922-1923, 1990-1991.

FA Cup: Winners: 1964, 1975, 1980. Runners-up: 1923.

Football League Cup: Runners-up: 1966, 1981.

European Competitions:

European Cup-Winners' Cup: 1964-1965 (winners), 1965-1966, 1975-1976 (runners-up), 1980-1981.

UEFA Cup: 1999-2000.

Intertoto Cup: (winners) 1999.

Wigan Athletic Football Club

Address:
JJB Stadium
Loire Drive
Newtown
Wigan, WN5 0UZ

Switch Board: 01942 774000
Ticket Office: 01942 774000
Website: www.wiganlatics.co.uk
Nickname: Latics
Year Formed: 1932
Record Attendance: 27,526 v Hereford U Dec, 1953
Record Receipts: £140,000 v Preston NE Apr, 2000
Record League Victory: 7-1 v Scarborough Mar, 1997
Record Cup Victory: 6-0 v Carlisle U Nov, 1934
Record Defeat: 1-6 v Bristol R Mar, 1990
Most Capped Player: Roy Carroll, Northern Ireland 9
Most League Appearances: Kevin Langley, 317

Record Transfer Fee Received:
£329,000 for Peter Atherton, Aug 1991

Record Transfer Fee Paid:
£700,000 for Lee McCulloch, Mar 2001

Capacity: 25,000   **Fanzine:** The Cockney Latic
Away Capacity: Varies **Unofficial site:** www.cockneylatic.co.uk
Disabled places: 100

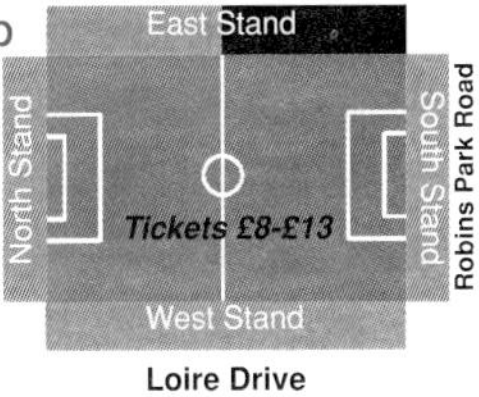

Last 5 Seasons:	Last 5 Managers:
1997: Div 3 - 1st	Ray Mathias (98-99)
1998: Div 2 - 11th	John Benson (99-00)
1999: Div 2 - 6th	Bruce Rioch (00-01)
2000: Div 2 - 4th	Steve Bruce (01)
2001: Div 2 - 6th	Paul Jewell (01-Pre)

Wigan Athletic Football Club

Rail: Wigan North Western 08457 484950

Bus: National Coach Enquiries 0870 6082608

Car: North: Exit the M6 at J27 and then turn left at the end of the slip road. Turn right at the T junction, signposted Shevington. After 1 mile turn left into Old Lane (signposted B5375) and the road winds through countryside for two miles. At the traffic lights turn right into Scot Lane and then take the 1st left for the stadium.

South, West: Exit the M6 at J25. At the end of the slip road turn left, signposted Wigan A49 for 1.8 miles to the complex junction. Turn left at the traffic lights filter into Robin Park Road. At the third set of lights turn right and follow the road round to the stadium.

East: Exit the M61 at J6 (signposted Chorley, A6027) and take the first exit at the roundabout. At the next roundabout take the first left into Chorley Road. After 0.3 miles turn right (signposted Wigan B5238) and then after 1.8 miles turn left at the roundabout (signposted Wigan B5238). 2.2 miles after the pub, turn right at the traffic lights. Turn left at the lights and then left again at the next lights. Follow the ring road and bear right into Caroline Street following signs for Orrell. Continue and pass Wigan pier and then go right at the next lights (after the Railway Bridge) into Robin Park Road. At the second set of lights go right to the stadium.

MY RATING

Date Visited: _____

Rating out of 10:

1 2 3 4 5 6 7 8 9 10

Note: _____

Wigan Athletic Football Club

Honours:

Football League: Division 3. Champions: 1996-1997. Division 4. Promoted (3rd) 1981-1982.

FA Cup: Best season: 6th rd, 1987.

Football League Cup: Best season, 4th rd, 1982.

Freight Rover Trophy: Winners: 1985.

Auto Windscreens Shield: Winners: 1999.

Wimbledon Football Club

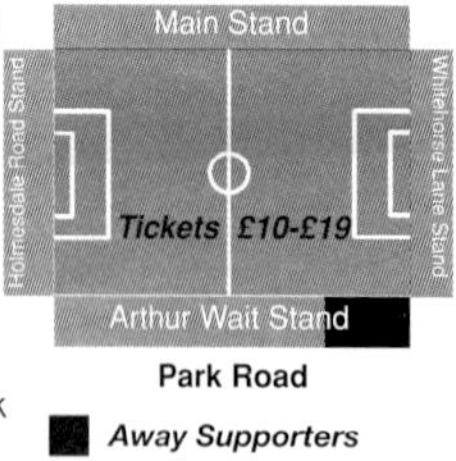

Address:
Selhurst Park
South Norwood
London, SE25 6PY
Switch Board: 020 8771 2233
Ticket Office: 020 8771 8841
Website: www.wimbledon-fc.co.uk
Nickname: The Crazy Gang
Year Formed: 1889
Record Attendance: 30,115 v Manchester U May, 1993
Record Receipts: £531,976 v Tottenham H Feb, 1999
Record League Victory: 6-0 v Newport Co Sep, 1983
Record Cup Victory: 7-2 v Windsor & Eton Nov, 1980
Record Defeat: 0-8 v Everton Aug, 1978
Most Capped Player: Kenny Cunningham, Republic of Ireland 33
Most League Appearances: Alan Cork, 430
Record Transfer Fee Received:
£7,000,000 for Carl Cort, Jul 2000
Record Transfer Fee Paid:
£7,500,000 for John Hartson, Jan 1999
Capacity: 26,297   **Fanzine:** Hoof the Ball Up
Away Capacity: 8,000
Unofficial site: www.weirdandwonderfulworld.com
Disabled places: 48

Tickets £10-£19

Park Road

Away Supporters

Last 5 Seasons:	Last 5 Managers:
1997: Prem - 8th	Ray Harford (90-91)
1998: Prem - 15th	Peter Withe (91)
1999: Prem - 16th	Joe Kinnear (92-99)
2000: Prem - 18th	Egil Olsen (99-00)
2001: Div 1 - 8th	Terry Burton (00-Pre)

Wimbledon Football Club

Travel:

Rail: Norwood Junction, Thornton Heath, Selhurst 08457 484950

Bus: National Coach Enquiries 0870 6082608

Car:

North: From M1, Take the A406 North Circular Road (West Bound) to Chiswick Roundabout. Take the third exit at the roundabout onto Chiswick High Road, then first left onto the A205 (signposted Kew). After two miles you reach a T-junction at which you should turn left (signposted Putney). Continue until the road merges with the A3, then a mile later turn right onto the A214. Once in Streatham turn right onto the A23. After 1 mile turn left onto Green Lane (B273) and at end turn left into High Street which runs into Whitehorse Lane. Selhurst Park is on your right.

East: From M25, take junction 4 which becomes the A21 and then A232. Follow the A232 (signposted Croydon) to Shirley then join A215 (signposted Norwood). In 2.2 miles turn left (B266) into Whitehorse Lane.

South: From the M25, take junction 8 and take the A23, following the signs for Thornton Heath. Turn right onto the A235. Once on the A235 turn immediately left onto the B266 Brigstock Road which becomes the High Street, then travel as if going North.

West: Take the M4 to Chiswick, then travel as if going North.

MY RATING

Date Visited: _____

Rating out of 10:

1 2 3 4 5 6 7 8 9 10

Note: _____

Wimbledon Football Club

Honours:

FA Premier League: Best season: 6th, 1993-1994.

Football League: Division 3. Runners-up: 1983-1984. Division 4. Champions: 1982-1983.

FA Cup: Winners: 1988.

Football League Cup: Semi-final: 1996-1997, 1998-1999.

League Group Cup: Runners-up: 1982.

Amateur Cup: Winners: 1963.

Runners-up: 1935, 1947.

Wolverhampton Wanderers Football Club

Address:
Molineux Stadium
Waterloo Road
Wolverhampton
WV1 4QR
Switch Board: 01902 655000
Ticket Office: 01902 653653
Website: www.wolves.co.uk
Nickname: The Wolves
Year Formed: 1877
Record Attendance: 61,315 v Liverpool Feb, 1939
Record Receipts: £319,141 v Arsenal Jan, 1999
Record League Victory: 10-1 v Leicester C Apr, 1938
Record Cup Victory: 14-0 v Cresswell's Brewery Nov, 1886
Record Defeat: 1-10 v Newton Heath Oct, 1892
Most Capped Player: Billy Wright, England 105
Most League Appearances: Derek Parkin, 501
Record Transfer Fee Received:
£5,000,000 for Ade Akinbiyi, Jul 2000
Record Transfer Fee Paid:
£3,000,000 for Ade Akinbiyi, Sep 1999
Capacity: 28,525   **Fanzine:** A Load of Bull
Away Capacity: 3,000 **Unofficial site:** www.thewolvessite.co.uk
Disabled places: 164

Last 5 Seasons:	Last 5 Managers:
1997: Div 1 - 3rd	Graham Turner (86-94)
1998: Div 1 - 9th	Graham Taylor (94-95)
1999: Div 1 - 7th	Mark McGhee (95-98)
2000: Div 1 - 7th	Colin Lee (98-00)
2001: Div 1 - 12th	David Jones (01-Pre)

Wolverhampton Wanderers Football Club

Travel:

Rail: Wolverhampton 08457 484950

Bus: National Coach Enquiries 0870 6082608

Car:

North, South, East:

Take the M6 to junction 10 and then take the A454 all the way into Wolverhampton. On reaching the traffic island that intersects with the ring road, turn right. As you approach the 2nd set of lights look for the signs for football parking. The ground is over the 2nd set of lights on the right.

West:

M54 to J2. Turn right onto the Stafford Road (A449) and continue until you see the Goodyear factory, go over the next two roundabouts until you get to the Five Ways roundabout. Take the third exit into Waterloo Road and the ground is 200 Meters on the left.

MY RATING

Date Visited: _____

Rating out of 10:
1 2 3 4 5 6 7 8 9 10

Note: _____

Wolverhampton Wanderers Football Club

Honours:

Football League: Division 1. Champions: 1953-1954, 1957-1958, 1958-1959. **Runners-up:** 1937-1938, 1938-1939, 1949-1950, 1954-1955, 1959-1960. **Division 2. Champions:** 1931-1932, 1976-1977. **Runners-up:** 1966-1967, 1982-1983. **Division 3 (N). Champions:** 1923-1924. **Division 3. Champions:** 1988-1989. **Division 4. Champions:** 1987-1988.

FA Cup: Winners: 1893, 1908, 1949, 1960. **Runners-up:** 1889, 1896, 1921, 1939.

Football League Cup: Winners: 1974, 1980.

Texaco Cup: Winners: 1971.

Sherpa Van Trophy: Winners: 1988.

European Competitions:

European Cup: 1958-1959, 1959-1960. **European Cup-Winners' Cup;** 1960-1961.

UEFA Cup: 1971-1972 (runners-up), 1973-1974, 1974-1975, 1980-1981.

Wrexham Football Club

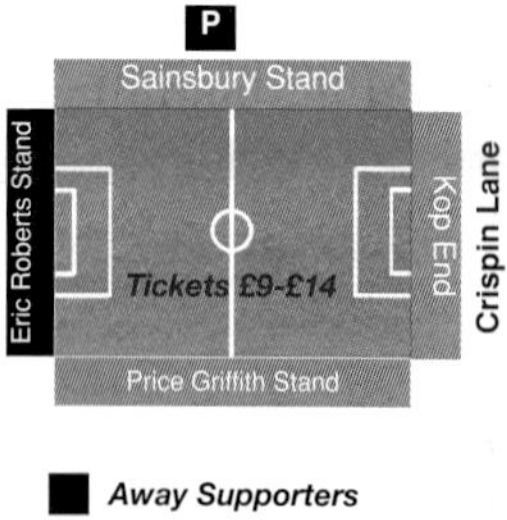

Address:
Racecourse Ground
Mold Road
Wrexham
LL11 2AH

Switch Board: 01978 262129
Ticket Office: 01978 262129
Website: www.wrexhamafc.co.uk
Nickname: The Robins
Year Formed: 1872
Record Attendance: 34,445 v Manchester U Jan, 1957
Record Receipts: £126,012 v West Ham Feb, 1992
Record League Victory: 10-1 v Hartlepool U Mar, 1962
Record Cup Victory: 11-1 v New Brighton Jan, 1934
Record Defeat: 0-9 v Brentford Oct, 1963
Most Capped Player: Joey Jones, Wales 29
Most League Appearances: Arfon Griffiths, 592
Record Transfer Fee Received:
£800,000 for Bryan Hughes, Mar 1997
Record Transfer Fee Paid:
£210,000 for Joey Jones, Oct 1978
Capacity: 15,500   **Fanzine:** Red Passion - The One and Only
Away Capacity: 3,000 Unofficial site: www.red-passion.com
Disabled places: Varies

Last 5 Seasons:	Last 5 Managers:
1997: Div 2 - 8th	Mel Sutton (81-82)
1998: Div 2 - 7th	Bobby Roberts (82-85)
1999: Div 2 - 17th	Dixie McNeil (85-89)
2000: Div 2 - 11th	Brian Flynn (89-01)
2001: Div 2 - 10th	Joey Jones (Caretaker)

Wrexham Football Club

Travel:

Rail: Wrexham General 08457 484950

Bus: National Coach Enquiries 0870 6082608

Car:North,West: Take the A483 from Chester to Wrexham to the junction with the A541. Branch left and at the roundabout follow signs for Mold. At the T-junction turn right into Regent Street which leads into Mold Road. Mold Road will then lead to the ground.

South: From the M6 junction 10A take the M54. Follow this road until it becomes the A5. Pass Shrewsbury and Oswestry and then join the A483 towards Wrexham. Leave the A483 at the junction of the A541 Mold road. The ground is 300 yards from this junction (on the A541) towards Wrexham town centre.

MY RATING

Date Visited: _____

Rating out of 10:

1 2 3 4 5 6 7 8 9 10

Note: _____

Honours: Football League: Division 2. Best season: 7th, 1997-1998. Division 3. Champions: 1977-1978. Runners-up: 1992-1993. Division 3 (N). Runners-up: 1932-1933. Division 4. Runners-up: 1969-1970.

FA Cup: Best season: 6th rd, 1974, 1978, 1997. Football League Cup: Best season: 5th rd, 1961, 1978. Welsh Cup: Winners: 23 times. Runners-up: 22 times. FAW Premier Cup: Winners: 1998, 2000. European Competitions: European Cup-Winners' Cup: 1972-1973, 1975-1976, 1978-1979, 1979-1980, 1984-1985, 1986-1987, 1990-1991, 1995-1996.

Wycombe Wanderers Football Club

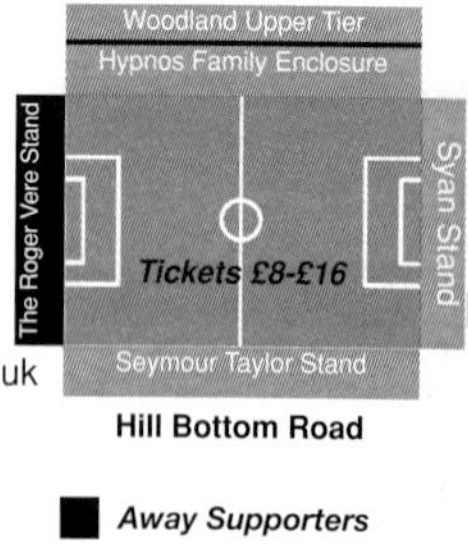

Address:
Adams Park
Hillbottom Road
Sands
High Wycombe, HP12 4HJ
Switch Board: 01494 472100
Ticket Office: 01494 441118
Website: www.wycombewanderers.co.uk
Nickname: The Chairboys
Year Formed: 1887
Record Attendance:
9,650 v Wimbledon Feb, 2001
Record League Victory: 5-0 v Burnley Apr, 1997
Record Cup Victory: 5-0 v Hitchin T Dec, 1994
Record Defeat: 0-5 v Walsall Nov, 1995
Most Capped Player: Nil
Most League Appearances: Dave Carroll, 290
Record Transfer Fee Received:
£375,000 for Keith Scott, Nov 1993
Record Transfer Fee Paid:
£220,000 for Sean Devine, Apr 1999
Capacity: 10,000   **Fanzine:** One-One
Away Capacity: 2,000 **Unofficial site:** www.chairboys.co.uk
Disabled places: 50

Last 5 Seasons:	Last 5 Managers:
1997: Div 2 - 18th	Martin O'Neill (90-95)
1998: Div 2 - 14th	Alan Smith (95-96)
1999: Div 2 - 19th	John Gregory (96-98)
2000: Div 2 - 12th	Neil Smilie (98-99)
2001: Div 2 - 13th	Lawrie Sanchez (99-Pre)

Wycombe Wanderers Football Club

Travel:

Rail: High Wycombe
08457 484950

Bus: National Coach
Enquiries 0870 6082608

Car:

From all Directions:

Exit the M40 at junction 4 and take the A4010 (John Hall Way) signposted Aylesbury. Cross over three mini roundabouts into New Road, continue downhill to two mini roundabouts at the bottom. Turn sharp left at the first roundabout into Lane End Road and turn right at the next mini roundabout into Hillbottom Road. Continue through the Industrial Estate to Adams Park at the end.

MY RATING

Date Visited: _____

Rating out of 10:
1 2 3 4 5 6 7 8 9 10

Note: _____

Honours:

Football League: Division 2. Best season: 6th, 1994-1995.

FA Amateur Cup: Winners: 1931.

FA Trophy: Winners: 1991, 1993.

GM Vauxhall Conference: Winners: 1992-1993.

FA Cup: Semi Final 2001.

Football League Cup: Never beyond 2nd round.

York City Football Club

Address:
Bootham Crescent
York
YO30 7AQ

Switch Board: 01904 624447
Ticket Office: 01904 624447
Website: www.ycfc.net
Nickname: The Minstermen
Year Formed: 1922

Record Attendance: 28,123 v Huddersfield T Mar, 1938
Record Receipts: £63,680 v Manchester U Oct, 1995
Record League Victory: 9-1 v Southport Feb, 1957
Record Cup Victory: 6-0 v South Shields Nov, 1968
Record Defeat: 0-12 v Chester Feb, 1936
Most Capped Player: Peter Scott, Northern Ireland 7
Most League Appearances: Barry Jackson, 481
Record Transfer Fee Received:
£1,000,000 for Jonathan Greening, Mar 1998
Record Transfer Fee Paid:
£140,000 for Adrian Randall, Dec 1995
Capacity: 9,534   **Fanzine:** None
Away Capacity: 3,500 Unofficial site: www.yorkcityfc.co.uk
Disabled places: 25

Last 5 Seasons:	Last 5 Managers:
1997: Div 2 - 20th	John Bird (88-91)
1998: Div 2 - 16th	John Ward (91-93)
1999: Div 2 - 21st	Alan Little (93-99)
2000: Div 3 - 20th	Neil Thompson (99-00)
2001: Div 3 - 17th	Terry Dolan (00-Pre)

York City Football Club

Travel:

Rail: York 08457 484950

Bus: National Coach Enquiries 0870 6082608

Car:

South:

Come off the A1 at junction 45 and head onto the A64 signposted for York. When you reach York, join the A1237 Ring Road and continue on it until you reach the junction with the A19. Take the A19 towards York City Centre and keep going until you get to a pub called the Burton Stone Inn, turn left. Continue until you get to the military barracks, turn right and the ground is in front of you.

North:

Follow the A1 and A1M to the A59. Continue on the A59 until you cross a railway bridge. Two miles after this turn left into Water End, and at the next T-junction turn right (signposted City Centre). Continue for a further half mile and then turn left into Bootham Crescent.

Honours:

Football League: Division 3. Promoted: 1973-1974 (3rd). Division 4. Champions: 1983-1984.

FA Cup: Semi-finals: 1955.

Football League Cup: Best season, 5th round, 1962.

MY RATING

Date Visited: _____

Rating out of 10:

1 2 3 4 5 6 7 8 9 10

Note: _____

My Top 20 Grounds Visited

	Ground Visited	Rating
1		
2		
3		
4		
5		
6		
7		
8		
9		
10		
11		
12		
13		
14		
15		
16		
17		
18		
19		
20		

Top 20 Grounds Visited

Please fill in your details below, tear out and send to:

FANFARE FOOTBALL GUIDE
5th Floor
Goldsmith House
137-141 Regent Street
London W1B 4HZ

Name _____

Address _____

_____

_____

Telephone _____

Club supported _____

Comment
What other information would you like to see in this guide?

notes

notes

notes

notes

notes

notes

notes

notes